Grantsmanship
&Fundraising

· F U N D A M E N T A L S ·

Guidelines for Human and Leisure Services Professionals

S. Harold Smith, Ph.D.
Kent State University

Daniel McLean, Ph.D.
Indiana University

Roger C. Coles, Ed.D.
Central Michigan University

Edited by Dr. Tom Jones

AALR

American Association for Leisure and Recreation
1900 Association Drive
Reston, VA 20191

A Project of the American Association for Leisure and Recreation
An Association of the
American Alliance for Health, Physical Education, Recreation, and Dance

ISBN# 0-88314-854-4

Purposes of the American Alliance for Health, Physical Education, Recreation, and Dance

The American Alliance is an educational organization, structured for the purposes of supporting, encouraging, and providing assistance to member groups and their personnel throughout the nation as they seek to initiate, develop, and conduct programs in health, leisure, and movement-related activities for the enrichment of human life.

Alliance objectives include:

- Professional growth and development – to support, encourage, and provide guidance in the development and conduct of programs in health, leisure, and movement-related activities which are based on the needs, interests, and inherent capacities of the individual in today's society.

- Communication – to facilitate public and professional understanding and appreciation of the importance and value of health, leisure, and movement-related activities as they contribute toward human well-being.

- Research – to encourage and facilitate research which will enrich the depth and scope of health, leisure, and movement-related activities; and to disseminate the findings to the profession and other interested and concerned publics.

- Standards and guidelines – to further the continuous development and evaluation of standards within the profession for personnel and programs in health, leisure, and movement-related activities.

- Public affairs – to coordinate and administer a planned program of professional, public, and governmental relations that will improve education in areas of health, leisure, and movement-related activities.

- To conduct such other activities as shall be approved by the Board of Governors and the Alliance Assembly, provided that the Alliance shall not engage in any activity which would be inconsistent with the status of an educational and charitable organization as defined in Section 501©(3) of the Internal Revenue Code of 1954 or any successor provision thereto, and none of the said purposes shall at any time be deemed or construed to be purposes other than the public benefit purposes and objectives consistent with such educational and charitable status.

Bylaws, Article III

American Association for Leisure and Recreation • 1900 Association Drive • Reston, VA 20191-1598
Phone: (703) 476-3472 • Fax: (703) 476-9527 • www.aahperd.org/aalr/aalr-main.html

Table of Contents

Chapter 1 – Introduction 1

    Criteria for Successful Philanthropy and Fund Raising Development 3

    Beginning Guidelines and Questions 3

Chapter 2 – Project Development 5

    Six Steps to Successful Project Development 7

    Proposal Components 7

    Making The Proposal Competitive 7

    Chapter Summary 9

Chapter 3 – Steps One and Two: Idea Formulation and Identification of External Sources ... 11

    Idea Formulation/Abstract 13

    Budget Summary 13

    Identification of External Sources 14

        Federal and State Governments 14

        Foundations 17

        Corporations 19

    External Sources: Some Important Differences 21

    Case Study – City of Cedar Rapids 22

    Chapter Summary 24

Chapter 4 – Step Three: Writing the Proposal 27

    The Proposal Writing Process 29

    Institutional Support 29

    Writing Approach 30

        Title Page 31

        Table of Contents 32

        Proposal Narrative 32

        Budget Preparation 38

            Line Item Budget 38

            Budget Narrative/Addendum 45

        Appendix 45

    Chapter Summary 46

Chapter 5 – Steps Four, Five and Six:
       Proposal Submission, Proposal Acceptance or Rejection, Project Management   47

    Introduction 49

    Proposal Submission 49

    Proposal Acceptance or Rejection 50

    Project Administration 50

    Chapter Summary..51

Chapter 6 – Bond/Millage Campaigns   53

    Introduction 55

    Pre-Campaign Feasibility Study...55

    Five Communication Tips 56

    Committees and Tasks 57

    Proposed Timeline 59

Chapter 7 – Fund Raising and Development   61

    Overview of Fund Raising and Development 63

    The Annual Fund 63

Appendices   67

    Appendix A – Sample RFAs/RFPs..67

        Governmental – Community Partners for Healthy Farming Intervention (CDC) 69

        Foundation – The James S. McDonnell Foundation 74

    Appendix B – Sample Grant Applications 79

        Operation Lifeline Proposal..79

        Assessing Functional Fitness in Sedentary and Physically Active Older Persons:
        An International Collaborative Research Project 89

Tables and Figures

Tables

Table 1 – Major Components of a Project Proposal 8

Table 2 – Comparison of External Funding Sources 16

Table 3 – List of Sources for External Funding Agencies 24

Figures

Figure 1 – Decision Tree for Proposal Pre-Assessment 4

Figure 2 – Six Steps to Proposal Development 7

Figure 3 – Sample Abstract 13

Figure 4 – Sample Budget Summary Form 14

Figure 5 – Sample Letter of Inquiry 19

Figure 6 – Sample Title Page 31

Figure 7 – Sample Project Summary 33

Figure 8 – Sample Proposal Introduction 34

Figure 9 – Sample Needs Statement 35

Figure 10 – Sample Project Objectives 36

Figure 11 – Sample Budget 40

Figure 12 – Sample Budget Narrative/Addendum 42

Figure 13 – Sample Budget 85

Figure 14 – The Physical Functioning Continuum 90

Chapter 1

Introduction

Criteria for Successful Philanthropy and Fund Raising Development

With tight budgets and continued need for strict financial accountability, many public and most private human service agencies are searching to identify external resources to assist in the operation and expansion of their programs and the development and renovation of their facilities. Philanthropy and Fund Raising is the systematic process for the development and acquisition of these resources from the formulation of the initial idea through the administration of the sponsored project. Although the process may appear to be complex, it is really quite simple when one becomes familiar with the mechanics and process of external support development. The seasoned individual understands that the same process and mechanics are used in applying for money ("fund raising", "grant writing", "grant seeking") as with any other type of resource such as land, building materials, computer equipment, volunteer labor, etc.

The focus of this material is on human service and leisure service professionals in the public and non-profit sectors, so that they may understand and find confidence in the process of philanthropy and fund raising. It is important to note that although examples used in the book relate mainly to leisure, parks, and recreation, the application of the concepts work equally as well in education, health, human or social services settings. The approach is a simple one, thus the name: **Philanthropy and Fund Raising Fundamentals.**

Beginning Guidelines and Questions

As the development process is initiated it is important to consider the following basic principles:

1. People give to people. Personal contact greatly enhances the potential for success.

2. Resource development is an art that is learned, not a science to be mastered.

3. The first and best place to look for external funding support is close to home.

4. Resource development begins with a good idea.

In addition, here are some questions that need to be answered before actually beginning the development of the proposal. Answering these questions early in the process can save much time, effort, and frustration later.

1. Are the chances of your proposal being funded great enough to be worth your time and effort?

Although you may not really know your chances, you should be aware that the great majority of proposals are not accepted on their first or second submittal. It is estimated, for example, that seventy-five percent of grant proposals are rejected on their first submission. This is not hard to understand when one realizes that for every proposal accepted, there may be as many as thirty other proposals submitted. Once an award is given, however, the chances of renewing the award or obtaining another one greatly increases — some say as much as eighty (80%) percent.

It takes time and effort to complete and submit a proposal and one should do everything possible to determine the benefit/cost relationship before beginning. If, for example, it will cost $900 in time, staff resources, and expenses to prepare an application for a $1,500 award, one needs to give serious consideration to the overall worth of the grant if awarded.

2. Is your proposal in harmony with your personal and professional goals, and does it meet the philosophy and goals of your agency?

Individuals and organizations must be very careful not to become involved in opportunities that are not consistent with their personal and professional goals. When an individual or organizational provider has the potential of giving tens of thousands or even millions of dollars it is easy to forget purpose and mission.

3. Why are you undertaking this adventure? Are you being honest and realistic with yourself and your agency?

Sometimes the best dreams can become the greatest nightmares. Is the problem you seem to be facing real or is it only perceived? Many times it is felt that receiving a project award will solve all problems

when in fact it may only compound them. Because of the time, effort, and commitment in the preparation and submission of a good proposal you must always be completely honest and realistic in your decision making process.

4. Have you shared your idea with other key people?

Conventional wisdom suggests including a number of people in the early "idea" stage of the fund seeking process. Especially be certain to include individuals who will challenge the process, people who see the world differently then you.

Figure 1 represents a decision tree that should help as you successfully answer these questions.

Figure 1: Decision Tree for Proposal Pre-Assessment

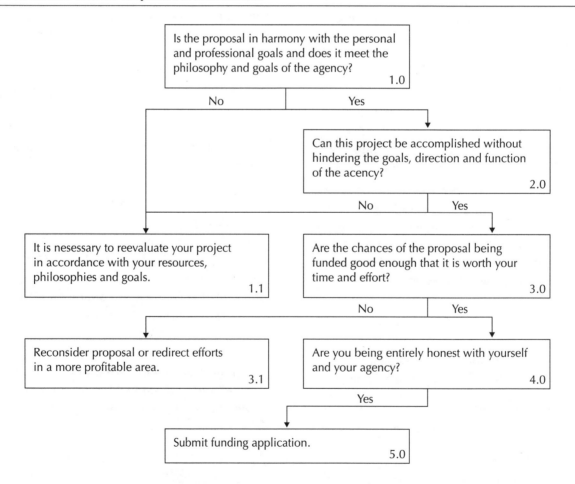

Chapter 2

Project Development

Six Steps to Successful Project Development

Philanthropy and fund raising is a skill *and* an art. This chapter presents the six steps in this developmental process including the major components of a proposal with suggestions on how to make a proposal more competitive. Each of these brief discussions serves as an introduction to information that will be developed in more detail later in the text.

The proposal development process flows through six interrelated steps. Successful completion of each step leads naturally to the next succeeding step. This natural flow process is depicted in Figure 2. Succeeding chapters will discuss each of these major steps in some detail.

Proposal Components

Generally all proposals submitted, whether large or small, should include each of the major proposal components. In many cases, the identified funding source provides an application packet covering each of the major component areas. When a packet is provided, follow its directions and answer its questions in detail. In cases where a formal application packet is not required or when the majority of the proposal is written before the funding source is identified, addressing each of the proposal components will assure a complete project proposal. Each of these major components is introduced in Table 1. A detailed discussion of each of the component areas is provided in a later chapter with samples provided from actual funding applications (see Appendix B).

Making The Proposal Competitive

The following checklist will help make your proposal more competitive and your preparation task easier. Successful resource developers soon learn to use their own style and approach while incorporating these ideas into proposal writing.

- Have you followed the application procedures carefully, addressed every criterion, answered every question, and given it a thorough review?

- Is your proposal neat, clean, and readable with no misspelled words?

- Have all of the related application forms been completed in detail?

Figure 2. Six Steps to Proposal Development

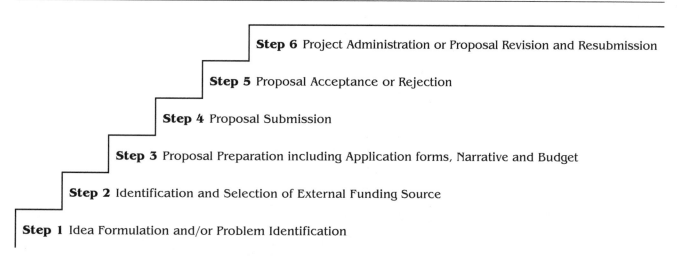

Step 6 Project Administration or Proposal Revision and Resubmission

Step 5 Proposal Acceptance or Rejection

Step 4 Proposal Submission

Step 3 Proposal Preparation including Application forms, Narrative and Budget

Step 2 Identification and Selection of External Funding Source

Step 1 Idea Formulation and/or Problem Identification

Table 1. Major Components of a Project Proposal

Component Area	*Component Specifics*
I. Abstract and Budget Summary	A. one page introduction to project B. summary of project budget
II. Introduction	A. who is the submitting agency B. your agency vision, mission, experiences, accomplishments & community support C. establish program and financial credibility
III. Problem/Need Statement	A. succinct statement of problem & expected outcomes B. data to identify and clarify problem or need C. why this project is important D. reasons you should be funded
IV. Objectives	A. stated in relation to problem/need B. stated in performance/outcomes terms, are specific, time oriented and measurable
V. Methods	A. timelines tied to objectives B. plan or action C. program design, interrelationship of project components D. identifiable "*deliverables*"
VI. Evaluation	A. process oriented B. product oriented C. external review D. internal review
VII. Budget	A. honest and realistic B. each component identified by line item C. identification of matching funds, local and/or coalition contributions D. no surprises or secrets E. within limits set by external resource guidelines
VIII. Summary	A. one page in length B. identifies of submitting agency C. states submitting agency credibility D. states problem/need E. gives project objectives and activities F. gives project costs
IX. Appendix	A. letters of support B. personnel vitae/resumes C. program brochure D. reports, data, and support documents E. job descriptions F. other requested data

- Have you included pictures, brochures, statistics, and/or support letters?

- Have you made the proposal readable using an outline form with underlining, section titles, short paragraphs and emphasis points?

- Have you identified joint use, multiple use or coalition arrangements including volunteers, facility and equipment sharing, and agency sponsorships?

- Are you aware of key words, target populations and identifiable phrases appropriate to your proposal reviewer and have these been used effectively in your presentation?

- Have you been honest in your presentation? Did you start with the important parts and avoid unsupported statements?

- Is your proposal as short and simple as possible?

- Have you been positive?

- Have other people reviewed and critiqued your proposal?

- Have you *met all deadlines*?

Chapter Summary

In summary, proposal development is a six-step process that can be followed in an easy, systematic pattern. The six steps are: idea formulation; identification of external source(s): proposal preparation; proposal submission; proposal acceptance or rejection; and project administration or proposal revision and resubmission. The successful proposal writer follows a basic outline in the development of the proposal that includes these main component areas: abstract and budget summary; introduction; problem/needs statement; objectives; methods; evaluation; budget; summary; and appendix. The use of these guidelines and procedures will make your proposal more successful in a highly competitive market.

Succeeding chapters review each of the proposal areas in more depth. Examples of each area are also provided for review. Each example is taken directly from an actual completed project application which may be reviewed in the Appendix. While a review of each of the individual areas is helpful, reading the full application will indicate the interrelationship of each proposal area in the successful project application.

Chapter 3

Steps One and Two:

Idea Formulation &

Identification of External Source(s)

Idea Formulation/Abstract

Some individuals or agencies which seek funding have already identified a need or developed an idea that would best be met by seeking external support. In many cases, however, this need or idea is in the mind of the key individual(s) involved, and not on paper. Since it is difficult to read a person's mind, it is a good practice to write a short abstract of the need/idea for funding that can be used as a focal point in searching for a funding source. This abstract can also be shared with colleagues and agency staff to obtain additional input, clarification, and support. It could be submitted to potential external sources for review as they are identified. The abstract need not be longer than two or three paragraphs and generally should be no longer than one typewritten page. The abstract should present the following characteristics of a fundable project.

- The proposal is new, innovative, and applies directly to your situation.

- The proposal has the potential to be cost effective and management efficient.

- Matching fund coalitions and local support are evident and the potential for long term support is high.

- There is documentation of a clear need.

- The time is right for this proposal.

A sample abstract is shown in Figure 3.

Budget Summary

With the abstract, a short budget summary indicating the projected cost of the primary components of the proposal should be developed. Because the amount of possible funding from an external source is not yet known, one should realistically project the cost of each of the main budget areas. Reviewing

these potential costs will also help clarify the financial reality of the idea. The budget summary should follow the format shown in Figure 4. In some cases, funding sources may provide monies for the development of capital expenditures as well. If this is the case, your budget summary should include this as a separate line item added to the format shown in Figure 4.

Figure 3. Sample Abstract

Operation Lifeline is a community-based program of St. Elizabeth Medical Center (SEMC). The purpose of this program is to provide a personal emergency response system which allows frail, elderly, and disabled individuals in Yakima County to remain living independently in their own homes despite advanced age, chronic medical problems, or social isolation.

For the past three years SEMC has sponsored the Operation Lifeline Program with initial funds from hospital guilds, civic and social organizations, and private donations. Through the provision of a telephone emergency alarm and response system, the program currently provides 54 individuals with a constant button which can be carried. If the individual shows unusual inactivity, the Lifeline system will automatically call for help to the 24-hour response base unit located in the SEMC Emergency Department.

At present levels, this emergency response system can service only a small fraction of eligible subscribers in Yakima County while a waiting list continues to grow. The number of applications for the Lifeline Service would be expected to increase greatly if publicity efforts were stepped up or if social service agencies were invited to refer their claims.

The St. Elizabeth Health Foundation is seeking funds to expand the Operation Lifeline Service so that the waiting list of eligible subscribers may be dissolved. We are asking the Foundation for $25,000 to provide the ongoing financial support necessary to operate and expand the program. This fund request will enable SEMC to meet a greater percentage of the need that is evident in the Yakima community. Specific funding includes the purchase of 30 additional Lifeline Units, one part-time personnel position to keep up with expansion demands, and operational costs not covered by the $8.00 monthly subscriber fees.

With a completed proposal abstract and budget summary, you are now ready to begin the search for the most appropriate funding source for the proposal. Depending on the amount of external funds desired and/or the complexity of your proposal, you may need to identify more than one potential external source. A discussion of the implications of sending the summary of the project proposal to more than one potential funding source is discussed in a succeeding chapter.

Identification of External Source(s)

You are now ready to begin the search for an external source. In general, there are three types of external sources: Federal and State Governments; Public and Private Foundations; and Corporations. A brief overview of the pros and cons of each of these potential external funding sources is found in Table 2.

Figure 4. Sample Budget Summary Form

Project	Total	Total Requested	Total Donated
A. *Direct Costs*			
1. Personnel Costs			
A. salaries & wages	$____	____	____
B. fringe benefits	$____	____	____
C. consultants &			
contract services	$____	____	____
Subtotal	$____	____	____
2. Non-Personnel Costs			
A. office rental	$____	____	____
B. equipment costs	$____	____	____
C. maintenance costs	$____	____	____
D. consumable supplies	$____	____	____
E. travel	$____	____	____
F. telephone	$____	____	____
G. other	$____	____	____
Subtotal	$____	____	____
B. *Indirect Costs*			
(Agency overhead, usually a negotiated % of total direct costs)	$____	____	____
Total Project Costs	$____	____	____

Federal and State Government(s)

Although not as financially liberal as in the 1970s and 1980s, federal and state governments continue to be the largest combined source of external funding dollars. Some experts say that federal and state governments "out give" foundations and corporations by as much as 80-90 times. The primary reason for this difference is that governments provide support in a tremendously wide range of areas. Today's awards from government sources tend to be for one-year project periods with possibilities of renewal or continuation up to three years if succeeding funding is received. Project awards are generally in the $50,000 to $100,000 range per project year. Government grants are very competitive. Sometimes several hundred applications are received for 15 to 25 grants. Because of this ratio, more than 80% of initial grant applications to government sources may be rejected. Once a governmental grant is obtained, however, there is an excellent chance of receiving additional funds in the future. Another serious consideration with government grants is that the red tape and application requirements are much greater than with most other types of external sources.

Government Source Listing. Publications are available that list the wide array of potential governmental funding sources. It should be noted that reviewing these resource listings is a tedious task because of the volumes of materials provided. The task may be simplified by acquiring the "Request for Application" (RFA)/"Request for Proposal" (RFP) that most governmental sources send to local agencies serving clientele related to the proposed requirements.

The primary government resource listings are:

- *Catalog of Federal Domestic Assistance*

- *Commerce Business Daily*

- *Federal Grants and Contracts Weekly*

- *Federal Grants Reporter*

- *Federal Register*

- *The Guide to Federal Assistance for Education*

- *United States Government Manual*

Ordering information for each of these resources is found in Table 3 at the end of this chapter. It is also important to note that most, if not all, of these resources are available on the world wide web. Accessing them through the world wide web is generally easier and less expensive at **http://www.caprep.com/fedreg.htm**. (Please note that URLs frequently change.)

Most of these publications are very detailed and take considerable time to review for specifics. The following suggestions will aid in the effective use of these resources.

1. *Using the catalogs and guides.*

    A. Use the indices to locate general information areas. They will provide, for example, different categories of funding sources such as recreation, human services, capital funds, and so on.

    B. Examine the selected area thoroughly. It is important to identify key words and/or target populations. Use these key words to cross-reference and expand the list of potential sources. List all of the alternative key words you can identify. Sometimes the publication lists key words. Target population terms frequently change based on current terminology. Government may be the initiator of new terms for target populations or may lag behind. Use both older and current terms for target populations.

C. Recognize the limitations of the publication. Most publications identify the sources upon which they draw. As you become familiar with the catalogs and guides some will be more helpful than others.

D. It is absolutely essential to follow up each possible funding source with a personal contact. The personal contact provides feedback about appropriate levels of funding and correct application procedure.

2. *Using the* Federal Register *to obtain information pertaining to grants.* **http://www.epa.gov/fedrgstr/**

    A. Begin by locating the notice of intent. This provides a list of RFAs/RFPs (see Appendix A) that the federal government will be seeking.

    B. The *Federal Register* should be used to identify proposed rules and definitions of terms that are important in preparation of proposals.

    C. The *Federal Register* identifies final regulations used in submission of proposal applications.

3. *Using the* Commerce Business Daily *to obtain announcements pertaining to potential government contracts.*

    A. The *Commerce Business Daily* lists RFAs/RFPs (see Appendix A) announced by the government. It lists the agency, type of proposal, name of contact officer, and telephone number.

    B. The *Commerce Business Daily* lists a request for statement of capability.

    C. The *Commerce Business Daily* lists a notice of sole source negotiations.

Once a potential governmental funding source is located, it will help to make contact with the governmental agency or program involved to obtain additional information and clarification. This contact should be in person if the agency office is conveniently located or by letter, telephone, FAX, or e-mail if some distance away. Contact should be made with the Project Contact Officer listed in the resource information. It is the project contact officer's job to provide you with information regarding the project area so don't hesitate to make such contacts. Some reasons that you will want to contact this officer are:

1. to obtain clarification on the information provided in the written guidelines;

2. to obtain advance notice of new programs, proposal deadlines, the availability of new information, or future directions of this program;

3. to help establish your credibility;

4. to further assess the funding potential of your project.

Typical information that you can expect to receive from the project contact officer would be:

- information on future directions and interests of the funding agency;

- estimates of future deadlines not yet officially established;

- the latest information about the particular program for which you are applying;

- clarification of information provided in proposal guidelines including criteria used in the review process;

Table 2. Comparison of External Funding Sources

Pros	Cons
Federal and State Governments	
1. Large amount of funds available.	1. Competition very high.
2. Wide variety of funding areas.	2. Extensive detail expected in application process.
3. Multi-year funding possible.	3. Much red tape.
4. Once funded, second funding becomes much easier.	4. Very political.
Foundations	
1. Once funded, second funding becomes much easier.	1. Competition very high.
2. Foundations are often tailored to specific giving.	2. Time invested in proposal preparation may have low payback.
3. Local foundations can be very supportive of local organizations.	3. It is very time consuming to seek out foundations that match your agency's needs.
Corporations	
1. Potential for monies is high.	1. Requires a significant amount of time to make contacts.
2. Local small corporations can be big supporters.	2. May require tailoring proposal to potential provider.
3. Corporations seeking tax breaks look for potential projects.	3. May need to establish a non-profit foundation to receive donations.
4. Programs which enhance images are particularly attractive.	
5. Small corporations can be major givers.	

- reactions to specific proposal ideas;

- information on the clearinghouse review procedures and management circulars that pertain to this program;

- the ratio of projects funded to proposals received in previous grant years;

- an estimate of ratio of projects to be funded to proposals received for the current grant year;

- the range and average dollar amounts of past proposals and estimates of such amounts for upcoming proposal solicitations;

- lists of projects funded in previous years;

- detailed information on previously funded projects;

- the type of people who will constitute the proposal review panel;

- the overall goals of the agency and particular mandates they may have received from Congress;

- position statements and written statements of future program plans.

Upon receiving your call or letter, the project contact officer will send an application packet for the project area for which you have an interest. This packet will contain all necessary forms and directions to apply for this project. It is very important that you read these application materials carefully and follow the instructions and timelines precisely. If you do not, you will be immediately eliminated from consideration for a project award.

Foundations

Foundations are non-profit organizations that provide external support in specific areas that are selected by the foundation board of directors or benefactors. Locating promising foundations may require considerable time and research because of the large number of foundations in the United States and because each has its own interest area(s) in giving. Generally speaking, foundations are identified in the following manner.

1. *Public Foundations*

    A. *Large* – those foundations generally having assets of $1,000,000 or more. They usually serve a broad national geographic area, have broad interest areas, employ a professional staff, and have a high ratio of proposals received to proposals awarded.

    B. *Small* – those foundations generally having assets of less that $1,000,000. They usually limit their geographic area of service, tend to have limited areas of interest, and are often family oriented.

2. *Private Foundations*

    Those foundations typically having interests directly related to a company interest, employee interest, or private interest. Generally speaking, they are very limited in geographical area served and have relatively small assets when compared to large foundations.

3. *Community Foundations*

    Those foundations that carry the name of a community or geographical area. They are limited to the geographical area identified and usually have very limited assets.

Foundation Source Listing. The following resources are available for identifying potential foundations to provide external support. Ordering information for each of these resources is found in Table 3.

1. The Grantsmanship Center

2. The Foundation Center

  · *The Foundation Directory*

  · *The Foundation Grants Index*

  · *The Foundation National Data Book*

  · *The Foundation News*

  · *The Foundation Source Book.*

  · *The Foundation Source Book Profiles*

3. Directory of Research Grants

4. Chronicle of Philanthropy

5. IRS tax returns

6. State guides/directories for foundations and charitable trusts

Most of these resources are quite expensive and their value to any particular agency varies greatly. In some cases the resource may be very helpful while in others it may not. For this reason it would be wise to review each resource carefully before a decision to purchase is made. Most public libraries in large cities and the research libraries in many colleges and universities have these resources available for reference. As with government resources, the majority of these catalogs and directories are accessible through the World Wide Web, which is usually more convenient and far less expensive.

The Foundation Directory is probably the single best resource in identifying major foundations. It provides the following information on all of the large foundations in the country:

1. Location, including address.

2. Important people, including names of trustees, officers, donors, and contact officers.

3. Purposes, including current activities, interests, and special limitations.

4. Financial status, including expenditures, assets, income, number and amounts of grants awarded.

5. Geographic region served.

Contacting the Foundation. Once you have identified a foundation that may be interested in your proposal, you must make personal contact with them. In most cases this first contact is made by submitting a letter of inquiry to the foundation contact officer explaining your interest in their foundation and asking for additional information. This letter of inquiry should always be prepared on your agency letterhead and should be brief and to the point. Along with the letter of inquiry you should submit a professional looking copy of your proposal abstract and budget summary. With this initial information, the foundation can respond indicating whether your proposal appears to meet their foundation guidelines and limitations. A sample letter of inquiry is provided for your review in Sample 1.

After receiving a positive response from the foundation, you should set up either a personal or telephone interview with the foundation contact officer. It is much better to have a personal interview, but if time or distance makes this unreasonable, a telephone interview is an acceptable substitute. Having personal contact with the foundation can be invaluable in establishing your credibility. The following are some other reasons this interview is important:

1. to establish a relationship with the foundation;

2. to create an opportunity to sell yourself, your agency and your idea;

3. to obtain information on the particular interests of the foundation;

4. to assess the funding potential of your idea and to receive additional suggestions.

In setting up this interview, the following items should be remembered:

1. Be positive, convincing and enthusiastic, but not pushy.

2. Use the name of a well-known person from your agency, if possible, to help establish your credibility.

Figure 5. Sample Letter of Inquiry

July 26, 1998

James P. Shannon, Executive Director
General Mills Foundation
PO Box 1113
Minneapolis, MN 55440

Dear Mr. Shannon,

It is our understanding that the General Mills Foundation supports projects in the area of scholarships for students in nutrition and wellness. Enclosed is an abstract and budget summary of a project that the Ohio Park and Recreation Association (OPRA) would like to undertake in this area.

We ask that you review these materials and evaluate whether they meet your guidelines and standards. If, upon review, you feel that our project has potential for receiving support from your foundation, please send to us the necessary application materials for support consideration.

Thank you for your time and effort in our behalf. We look forward to hearing from you in the near future.

Sincerely,

Jane S. Johnson
Executive Director
(206) 786-1212

enclosure

3. Prepare for a brief 15-30 minute meeting, keeping your presentation short and simple.

4. Have a number of questions ready to ask during the interview but also be prepared to answer questions about your proposal.

5. *Be prepared!*

Remember, this information gathering opportunity will help you develop and focus your actual proposal to meet the requirements of the selected foundation.

Corporations

Commercial businesses and corporations may receive significant tax advantages by giving either "before tax" or "after tax" donations to charitable and non-profit organizations. If you are seeking support for a charitable or a non-profit organization you have the potential of receiving these donations directly. If you represent a governmental, public, or commercial organization these resources may not be available to you directly. In this case, it may be to your advantage to establish your own non-profit foundation so that you may be eligible for these types of donations. The procedures for establishing a non-profit organization can be easily obtained by contacting the Secretary of State office in your state and submitting the necessary paper work to the Internal Revenue Service (IRS). Currently, only about 1% of corporate donations is contributed to non-profit foundations. To better understand the potential of this area, reports show that commercial corporations gave more money to non-profit organizations than did foundations, an estimated total donation volume of $3.4 billion. Some estimate that recreation oriented sponsorship of this type across the

nation includes nearly 2,000 separate corporations that give over $850 million as program sponsors. Some development experts feel that these figures have the potential of being expanded by 400%.

Finding a Corporation. The single best resource for locating a corporation involved in this type of giving is the *Special Events Report* available for approximately $100 per year. A second excellent resource, especially in recreation, is the *Recreation Executive Report.* Ordering information for these and other corporation materials is found in Table 3.

In addition to a national search, a local investigation may locate corporations in your immediate area that are involved in corporate giving. Recruiting a local stockbroker or banker to be on your foundation board of directors may help to stay current with what corporations and businesses are doing in your locale. Realize that these individuals have professional confidences that they must keep, but in many cases they are very helpful in making suggestions as to the best potential corporate givers. In addition, it may be to your benefit to read *The Wall Street Journal, Fortune* and *Forbes* business magazines, *The Chronicle of Higher Education, Chronicle of Philanthropy,* your local business and economic paper, and your local newspaper to keep up with the business and economic climate in your locale.

Corporations tend to give sponsorship to programs that will enhance their image in local and national markets, that provide additional benefits to their employees or their families, or that will enhance the quality of living in those communities impacted by their employees. By keeping up with the local economic climate and by appealing to these needs of the corporate giver, you can often be successful in obtaining funds or resources. The corporation does not have to be large to give money or support. Ninety-four percent of the corporations that made

gifts to non-profit organizations gave $1,000 or less. Non-profit organizations can take full advantage of this type of giving by developing a simple plan of action that considers the following points.

1. Make a list of all the places your agency and staff spend their money.

2. Ask board members to also make a list of where they spend money.

3. Ask staff and board members to list every place they have worked either part of full-time over the past five to ten years.

4. Ask staff and board members to keep a card in their wallet or checkbook and each time they spend money during the next month list the name of the business that received their business.

5. Ask other organizations for the names of businesses and corporations that gave donations to them over the past five years.

6. Combine all of these lists into a single list of "potentials" where you, your staff, or your board members have spent money. Those businesses/corporations coming to the top of your lists should then be prioritized and contacted to determine their willingness to support your programs.

After establishing the list of businesses/corporations with which you do business, identify those you want to approach with your project, and decide who from your team would be your best contact persons. Do not be too concerned with competition from other groups; most successful commercial organizations are likely to give to a variety of worthy community causes.

Remember also that many commercial organizations can give resources other than money. You may be better served, for example, by asking for volunteer talent in specialty areas that you don't have in your agency. A top-notch advertising firm could be asked to design your public relations materials, to design the new logo for your department, or even provide T-shirts for your next special event. An accounting firm could give assistance with bookkeeping and auditing needs. Another group may want to take on a project activity as community service such as running your local tennis or golf tournament or by providing the manpower for your local Special Olympics meet. Many corporations encourage their employees to give volunteer time to worthy community projects.

Tax laws also allow commercial organizations to "write off" much of their equipment costs over several years. This means that they can choose to depreciate the value of their new equipment purchased during this time period, and then donate the equipment to your agency and take the current market value of the equipment off their taxable income. Since the technology of word processors, personal computers, and other typical office equipment is advancing at such a rapid pace, progressive corporations want the most up-to-date equipment and are often happy to donate their "old models" to you so that they can take advantage of the tax and technological advantages.

You may also be able to obtain office furniture when a company moves or redecorates. Inform board members and community advocates of your office and equipment needs and ask them to watch for opportunities for your agency to be first in line when a corporation needs to find a "charity" for its discards. St. Norbert College in DePere, Wisconsin has one of the best weight training facilities in the country because the Green Bay Packers use their facility for preseason training. Whenever the Packers update the weight equipment in their regular training facility, they

donate the "old" equipment to St. Norbert. The Kent Commons Community Center in Kent, Washington generate revenue each year because they negotiated through the Seattle Super Sonics to obtain the contract to provide NBA playing space for a part of each summer. Similar opportunities may be available in your community if you look for them.

External Sources: Some Important Differences

Additional information about the differences in external sources follows.

- Personal contact with officers of foundations and corporations is far more important than with government agencies.

- It is always a good practice to provide an abstract and budget summary when contacting a foundation or a corporation. Federal agencies, however, seldom request such information and seldom respond to it if submitted.

- Foundations and corporations tend to fund activities for which government support is not available.

- Foundations and corporations have much more flexibility in their funding procedures than do government agencies.

- Foundations and corporations tend to give greater emphasis to the uniqueness and quality of the project than do government agencies.

- Foundations and corporations generally have less detailed application procedures and guidelines, thus leading to shorter and less detailed proposals. Government application procedures are usually very detailed and filled with "red tape."

Case Study – City of Cedar Rapids

The following case study provides insights into how one organization pursued the grantseeking process. The first column is the case study. The case is interpreted and explained in the right hand column. Note how the different aspects of the case study are related back to the grantseeking process.

Cedar Rapids Case Study	Implications and Explanations
The Cedar Rapids Recreation Commission had provided community recreation opportunities for 65-years. About five years before a granting initiative was begun a new staff member was hired to provide aquatic supervision for the communities' six pools. During the off-season the position was involved in providing coordinating services for persons with disabilities. Because of the nature of the aquatic responsibilities it was unreasonable to expect that the individual could do more than provide some services during the fall to early spring. A conscious decision was made to collaborate rather than to initiate separate programming. There were several early successes in the program, the most important being the development of a multiple agency coordinating council that met on a monthly basis to discuss needs, resources, and actions. At one of these meetings one of the key organizations providing recreation services announced it was getting out of the recreation business.	Problems or issues often arise unexpectedly, as in this case study, and organizations are challenged to meet the need or resolve the problem. The Recreation Commission had provided some services to persons with disabilities, but there was not a recognized problem or need until the key provider announced they were withdrawing so they could concentrate their energies on their primary mission. The withdrawal of a service organization left a major gap in the provision of services to an identified under-served population.
This provided an immediate concern to the community and to the Recreation Commission. In the initial report from the aquatics supervisor, it was seen only as a problem. The Director and Assistant Director immediately, however, saw it as an opportunity and once they shared it with the aquatics supervisor, she too was excited. After several informal meetings it was determined that the Recreation Commission should take a more active role in the provision of recreation opportunities for individuals with disabilities. The best way to accomplish this was to create a new position that would focus wholly on persons with disabilities. Unfortunately the current operating budget did not allow for the addition of a new staff person. Discussions with the city auditor and appropriate concilperson suggested that no new money would be forthcoming for such a project. The cost of the position, supporting personnel and operation was estimated at $100,000 a year.	The perception of a problem or opportunity is in the eyes of the effected. As shown here, the aquatics supervisor was too close to the problem to see this solution. Her colleagues saw the issue from a different perspective. In identifying potential problems it is good to secure perspectives from several different people. In this case, the Recreation Commission, city council and other service providers were also brought in to help identify the problem and to secure their input.
The Director determined early on that six groups were essential to the success of the process. Those were individuals who would benefit from the service, the city council, the local granting foundation, the Recreation Commission (a policy setting board), other service providers for individuals with disabilities, and the recreation commission staff. Each has a unique role. The aquatics/special population supervisor was asked to go back to the other service providers and ask for their initial verbal support for a grant. The Director briefed the Recreation Commission and secured their initial support to move forward in the grantseeking process.	Note in this phase that no decision was made to link the problem's resolution with a particular grant-maker. Undoubtedly many grant proposals are initiated anticipating one or more grantmakers, but unless there is pre-agreement for funds, grantseekers should move forward in this phase assuming they may have to submit to multiple grantmakers.

continued from page 22

Cedar Rapids Case Study	Implications and Explanations
Simultaneously contact was made with the executive director of a local foundation that had previously been supportive of the community and the Recreation Commission. The purpose of these early conversations was to determine the willingness of the foundation to support the project and under what conditions. Additionally meetings were held with the councilperson with primary responsibility for the Recreation Commission and the mayor. The outcomes of these meetings provided the recreation staff with additional information as they strategized approaches to securing a grant.	The Recreation Commission was fortunate to have a local foundation willing to consider the grant. This is more common that might be expected. Many local foundations are committed to community projects, even when they are not identified as "community foundations." An important aspect of this grant proposal was the Director's multiple year relationship with the foundation executive director. It did not guarantee the grant, but it did increase the potential for its funding.
The recreation staff determined that the approach with the greatest potential to secure a new position was to write a five-year grant proposal that simultaneously committed the city and the local foundation to a shared responsibility. It was agreed that the city could, over a five-year period, gradually increase the operating budget to the Recreation Commission to cover the cost of a new position. Other service providers were committed to continue their current level of service.	The foundation, early on, made it clear that it would only support a grant if the other organizations maintained their current level of programming for persons with disabilities.
The final proposal, as submitted, asked for a five-year commitment beginning with $100,000 the first year, increasing the operating budget by 5% a year, and reducing the foundation's commitment by 20% each year until year 6 when it makes no contributions. The city was to increase its commitment by 20% until the city was funding 100%. As part of the proposal a requirement was included that required the Recreation Commission to continue to pursue other grant sources to support programs during the five-year grant period and following. This last portion was added to the proposal to allay funding concerns on the part of the city council. Attached to the proposal was a letter from the city council committing to the funding level. Each of the organizations who were currently involved in providing services also prepared letters of support and additionally committed to not reduce their programming level for persons with disabilities.	The final proposal followed a traditional format and had the city council agreement and support letters from other serviced providers as appendices.

The grant was awarded without restriction over a five-year period. Annual reports were made to the foundation regarding the budget.

Evaluation of the funded project involved three agencies. Semiannual evaluation reports were made to the foundation, city council and recreation commission. |

The following table depicts how the grant funding was to be distributed over the proposed five-year period.

Grant Funding Proposal for new Recreation Position

	Requested	Foundation Commitment	City Commitment
Year 1	$100,000	$100,000	$0
Year 2	$105,000	$84,000	421,000
Year 3	$110,250	$66,150	$44,100
Year 4	$115,763	$46,305	$69,458
Year 5	$121,551	$24,310	$97,241
Totals	**$552,563**	**$3290,765**	**$231,798**

- Foundations and corporations usually will accept a proposal at any time while government agencies have very specific application deadlines.

- Foundations and corporations rarely require the volume of forms and assurances that government agencies require.

- Foundations and corporations generally do not give reasons for proposal rejection and are under no legal obligation to do so. In most cases, government agencies are required to provide specific information on proposal rejection when *requested* to do so.

- Foundations and corporations tend to be more flexible about how awarded funds may be spent than are government agencies.

Chapter Summary

To summarize, a fundable idea is new and innovative, has a good potential of being cost efficient, will be supported by local funds, has a clear documented need, and is timely. In looking for potential external sources, start in your own locale, using local resources first and then considering regional, state, and national resources. Most, if not all, of the resource guides, catalogs, magazines, and newspapers which identify potential sources are available at the public library, through most college and university libraries and/or on the world wide web. Doing your homework "up front" in the identification and selection of the right funding source is time consuming, but will greatly improve the chances of your proposal being funded/supported.

Table 3. List of Sources for External Funding Agencies

Governmental Agencies

1. *Catalog of Federal Domestic Assistance*, Office of Management and Budget (published annually with periodic updates).
2. *Commerce Business Daily*, U.S. Department of Commerce (published on weekdays).
3. *Federal Grants and Contract Weekly*, Capitol Publications, Inc., 1300 N. 17th Street, Suite 1600, Arlington, VA 22209.
4. *Federal Grants Reporter*, Federal Grants Information Center, 1725 K Street, NW, Suite 200, Washington, D.C. 20006.
5. *Federal Register*, U.S. General Services Administration (published on weekdays). Available on the world wide web.
6. *The Guide to Federal Assistance for Education*, Wilborn Associates, Inc., 14 Thornwood Court, Clover, SC 29710.
7. *United States Government Manual*, U.S. General Service Administration.

All of the Federal publications listed are available from: Superintendent of Documents, Government Printing Office, Washington, D.C. 20402.

Foundations

1. The Grantsmanship Center, 1031 South Grand Ave., Los Angeles, CA 90015.
2. The Foundation Center, 79 Fifth Ave., New York, NY 10003.
3. *Directory of Research Grants*, Oryx Press, 2214 N. Central at Encanto, Phoenix, AR 85004.
4. Individual state guides or directories for foundations and charitable trusts are available through the Secretary of State or Attorney General office in most states. State library systems also may have them available.
5. IRS Tax Returns for selected private foundations are available through the state library system.

All Foundation Center publications are available at this address with the exception of *The Foundation Directory* and *The Foundation Grants Index*. These items are distributed by Columbia University Press, 136 South Broadway, Irvington, NY 10533.

Corporations

1. *Special Events Report,* 213 West Institute Place, Suite 303, Chicago, IL 60610.
2. *Recreation Executive Report,* PO Box 27488, Washington, D.C. 20038.
3. *The Chronicle of Higher Education,* 1255 23rd Street, N.W., Washington, D.C. 20037 *http://www.chronicle.com*
4. *The Chronicle of Philanthropy,* 1255 23rd Street N.W., Washington, D.C. 20037 *http://www.philanthropy.com*
5. *The Wall Street Journal* (local news stand).
6. *Fortune Magazine* (local news stand).
7. *Forbes Magazine* (local news stand).
8. IRS tax returns (state library system).
9. Local business and daily newspapers.

Other Possible Sources

1. Annual reports
2. Telephone directories
3. Newsletters
4. State and federal legislation

Information Services

There are a wide array of informational services available, most for a price. Several hundred dollars is not uncommon for their services. The value of a particular service to a given agency varies greatly. Some will find one of the services worth the cost while others will not. You should examine each of the agencies carefully before purchasing any. Again, many of the services and information are available through the world wide web. These sources are generally free or of nominal charge. Some of the services currently available are:

1. The Grantsmanship Center, 1030 South Grand Ave., Los Angeles, CA 90015.
2. The Foundation Center, 79 Fifth Ave., New York, NY 10003.
3. Foundation Research Service, Lawson Williams Associates, Inc., 39 East 51st Street, New York, NY 10022.
4. Taft Information System, Taft Products, Suite 600, 1000 Vermont Ave., NW, Washington, D.C. 20005.
5. The Oryx Press Grant Information System, The Oryx Press, 3930 East Camelback Road, Phoenix, AZ 85018.
6. *College and University Reporter,* Commerce Clearing House, Inc., 4025 W. Peterson, Chicago, IL 60646.
7. *Guide to Federal Assistance for Education,* New Century Education Corporation, 440 Park Avenue South, New York, NY 10016.

Helpful Web Sites

- Grant Writing – This site links the user to other sites that provide useful information and up-to-date news. *http://www.marymy.edu-hoegler/facres/grantit.html*
- Grant Proposal Writing Workshops – Posts a schedule by month and state for workshops that focus entirely on the proposal writing process. *http://www.tgci.com/training/prposal.htm*
- Grant Writing Grant Resource Site FUND – Grant writing links include: Writing the Cover Letter; Tips for Writing Grant Proposal; and Grant Writing Aids. The grant source sites include: The Foundation Center; Grants in Graduate Studies; and the Index of the U.S. Department of Education programs. *http://www.coba.wright.edu/bie/grants.htm*
- Guide to Grant Proposal Writing – This site was developed by the staff of the Library Development Bureau, New Jersey State Library affiliated with Thomas Edison State College. The contents include writing tips and examples of grant proposal sections. *http://www2.njstatelib.org/njlib/grhdtoc.htm*

NAHE, Winter, 1999

Chapter 4

Step Three:

Writing the Proposal

The Proposal Writing Process

The formal proposal writing process begins once the funding source has been identified, contacted, and application materials received. Writing the proposal is the biggest challenge. The energy expended on a well thought out, researched, and written proposal will improve immeasurably your chances of receiving an award. The proposal writing process involves three stages: 1. completion of all application forms and assurances; 2. writing the proposal narrative; and 3. developing and presenting a detailed line item budget. As you begin this process, consider the following suggestions.

1. Read the proposal guidelines carefully. Follow them explicitly. Have someone else proof your work.

2. Do the necessary preliminary work. Make contact with key people in supporting agencies/coalitions.

3. Discuss the proposal with the various local people and agencies that will be involved in the project. Get their reactions and approval.

4. Make early contact with the office/department in your agency that will be responsible for the administrative details of proposal submission and project fund management. In organizations where there are multiple departments involved it will be necessary to contact each of them (e.g., personnel, comptroller, city manager, etc.). Get answers to the following questions.

   A. What is the process within the agency for approving the submission of your proposal?

   B. What assistance can this office provide?

   C. How are matters such as clearinghouse reviews, federal assurances and compliance, and project fund accounting handled?

   D. How much time will be needed for your agency to process the proposal internally?

5. Begin by making an outline of the overall proposal components.

6. Get critical reactions to this initial outline from agency personnel and others who may be involved with the project.

7. As the proposal is being written, a careful review by these same people should be very helpful.

8. If various sections of your proposal are to be written by different people or departments, identify *one* person to take responsibility for integrating the sections and doing the final editing work.

9. When letters of support are required, be quite specific in indicating what is needed from the people writing them. Such letters are most important when another person or agency is expected to make a substantial commitment to your project.

Institutional Support

As you become involved in the proposal preparation process you will find that it is very difficult to do all of the work yourself. In most cases your agency can do a great deal to assist in the preparation of a good proposal. Depending on the size and nature of your organizational structure, this assistance may be either centralized or decentralized. In many cases the most effective approach is to centralize some assistance activities and decentralize others, depending on organizational function and strength. In any case, your proposal must show an organized and consistent approach to the funding source.

In one community the recreation department determined the need for an elevator to make their facility more accessible and began soliciting funding for this project. Several meetings with

a local foundation were established to determine potential support. Local business leaders were solicited in an effort to secure a broad base of support and to encourage foundation support for the project. The city, however, had just submitted another proposal to the same foundation for a sizable capital improvement. The city indicated that no resources were available for their contribution in this project but that the mayor would write a letter of support for the project request. The result was that neither proposal was funded by the foundation because of the lack of communication within the city government structure. This example emphasizes the importance of gaining institutional support before outside support is solicited.

The kinds of assistance agencies may provide during the proposal preparation process include:

1. help in developing appropriate expectations and scheduling the many steps that are part of the preparation process;

2. assistance in acquisition of necessary information;

3. assistance in writing and editing of the proposal;

4. seed money and/or matching resource support such as office space, equipment, secretarial support, technical assistance, etc.;

5. simplified processes for handling federal assurances, compliance, and clearinghouse review procedures;

6. budgetary assistance in determination of indirect costs and fringe benefit package percentages;

7. coordination with other proposals within the agency.

Writing Approach

Using a proper writing approach is extremely important. Proper grammar, sentence structure, and spelling are minimum expectations for any proposal. Consistency in presentation throughout the proposal is vital. It is very easy to be misunderstood by using terms or phrases that are familiar to you but may lead to confusion for the review team. An example of this lack of consistency would be using a term like "department," when in earlier material the agency was referred to as "The Washington State Department of Natural Resources" and this abbreviation has not been explained. A clear and more consistent writing technique would be to use either a reference word, acronym or abbreviation directly following the initial use of the full name or reference. Using the above example, Washington State Department of Natural Resources would be presented to the reader the first time, followed by (department) or (DNR). This alerts the reader that in further references to this term a reference word, acronym or abbreviation will be used in its place, i.e., Washington State Department of Natural Resources (DNR). This allows for greater efficiency because you do not have to use the cumbersome term "Washington State Department of Natural Resources" any longer.

As you consider your writing approach the following suggestions may be helpful.

1. Good organization and structure are basic to good writing.

2. Good structure begins with an outline that is visible and consistent throughout the proposal. A complete set of headings and subheadings are helpful in this regard.

3. Each section of the proposal should begin with an introductory statement, usually one sentence or one paragraph that explains what will be discussed in that section.

4. Each paragraph should begin with a good topic sentence.

5. Whenever possible each section should be concluded with a section summary.

6. There is no substitute for practice in writing. The more times you rewrite your proposal, the better it will become. Have others edit and critique your proposal.

Title Page

Most application packets include some type of title page or project application form. If they do not, it is usually to your benefit to provide one in your proposal. At a minimum, the title page should include the following information.

1. Project title: a short, imaginative description of your project.

Figure 6. Sample Title Page

PROJECT EXETRA

PROGRAM ASSISTANCE GRANT
FOR
EXTENDED EDUCATION IN THERAPEUTIC
RECREATION ADMINISTRATION

through
The Bureau of Education for the Handicapped
U.S. Office of Education

TITLE: PROJECT EXETRA

APPLICATION ORGANIZATION: University of Oregon
                            Eugene, Oregon 97403

INITIATOR: _____

                            S. Harold Smith, Ph.D., MTRS
                            Professor and Director
                            Center of Leisure Studies
                            Department of Recreation & Park Management
                            University of Oregon
                            Eugene, Oregon 97403
                            (503) 686-3602

AUTHORIZATION: _____

                            Aaron Novick, Dean
                            (503) 686-5128

FUNDING PERIOD: June 1, 1998 to May 31, 1999
                            (1st year of 3 year funding cycle)

TOTAL FUNDS: BEH/DPP Support Requested $101,593
                            University Support   99,878
                                         TOTAL: 201,471

2. Name of project director with address and telephone number(s).

3. Complete name of the submitting agency with the name/address of the contact officer, if different than the project director.

4. Beginning and termination dates of your project, inclusive.

5. Total funds requested.

6. Names, addresses and telephone numbers of other officers authorized to negotiate for or legally commit the submitting agency.

7. Signature of project director and all other authorizing officers.

The title page should be limited to one typed page of information. An example of a title page is provided in Sample 2.

Table of Contents

The table of contents identifies each of the major headings and subheadings by page number for quick identification and reference. If extensive Tables, Figures or Samples are used, a listing of each of these items should also be included. An example of a table of contents is provided in Sample 3.

Proposal Narrative

Summary

Most application formats call for a project summary to be included at the beginning of the proposal, frequently as a part of the proposal introduction. The project summary should not be written until the proposal narrative is completed. This often confuses the beginning writer because it is placed at the beginning of the project proposal.

It is also often confused with the proposal abstract that is written as a preliminary step in the formulation of the project idea.

The project summary is just that: a summary of the actual proposal as it is written. It is placed at the beginning of the proposal so the review panel may have an overview of what to expect as they review the proposal. The project summary is limited to one page or less and should *not* include information given in the title page. It should include key information from each of the major sections of the proposal. In essence, anyone interested in your proposal should be able to read the project summary and know exactly what it is you are attempting to do. An example of a project summary is found in Sample 4.

Introduction

The introduction begins the narrative portion of the proposal. It must introduce your agency and establish agency credibility. In most application formats, the introduction is limited to one to five pages and should be as brief as possible while providing the information necessary to establish your credibility. When writing the introduction the following information must be addressed.

Identification of the agency applying for the funds, including submitting agency purposes, goals, programs, activities, and clients/constituents. This can often be accomplished by providing a copy of the agency public relations brochure. If this is done, the information should be summarized in the introduction with a copy of the actual brochure being placed in the proposal appendix for additional review.

Evidence of submitting agency accomplishments including statistical support and endorsements of these accomplishments by reputable sources.

Direct quotes from clients, community advocates or involved professionals create stronger credibility.

Identification of qualifications of the submitting agency and its staff to accomplish the activities for which funds are being requested. This also helps to establish credibility in fiscal management, program provision, and project administration.

Identification of the organizational structure of the proposal, which leads logically to the problem/ needs statement.

Establishment of the unique role being addressed in this particular problem/need.

An example of a proposal introduction is found in Sample 5.

Problem/Need Statement

The problem/need statement identifies and documents the need(s) to be met or the problem(s) to be addressed through this project. This section must establish the problem or need as significant enough for the funding source to provide support for it. The problems/needs described must be consistent with the philosophy and goals of both the funding source and the submitting agency and must directly relate to the objectives and activities described within the proposal.

The problem/need statement should be reasonable, not trying to solve all possible problems in a single project. Whenever possible, problems/ needs should be substantiated with specific data and supported by statements from recognized

Figure 7. Sample Project Summary

The Washington State Department of Game (DOG) manages the Oak Creek Wildlife Management Area, located north of Yakima, Washington. Every winter, hundreds of elk migrate to the Oak Creek area to feed on hay provided by DOG and volunteers. Thousands of Washington residents visit the area to view the elk as well as other wildlife such as bighorn sheep and deer. The only facilities at the site are employee housing and feed barns.

The DOG has proposed building an environmental education/information center at the Oak Creek Wildlife Management Area. The center would provide visitor information and school education programs as well as providing restroom facilities. The center would allow visitors to view the elk without standing outside in the snow. The center would be used throughout the year for educating the public about Washington's wildlife, particularly those species found in the Yakima region.

There is a need for a public facility of this caliber in the Yakima region as there are currently no facilities for environmental education in this area. Residents of Yakima county and the lower valley would be the prime user groups. The public in general would also be served through the environmental education and wildlife management programs.

The center project would be administered through the state Inner Agency Council and the regional manager for DOG in the Yakima region. Regional and state staff and specialists would operate the proposed center.

authorities and program constituents. If the problem/need is substantially out of the ordinary, there is an even greater necessity for providing quality supporting data. The problem/need should be stated in terms of the constituents' problems/needs and should be developed with input from the constituents and/or program beneficiaries.

Problem/need statements should reflect an understanding of related research or other projects currently functioning or being designed to resolve this problem and should make no unsupported assumptions or generalizations. If the project is a research proposal, this section must also include a review of related research/literature. In the case of a research proposal, the needs section must be a substantial piece of scholarly work that goes beyond the compilation of an annotated bibliography. The needs section must make a compelling case for the importance of the project. An example of a problem/need statement is found in Sample 6.

Objectives

The purpose of the objectives section is to establish the benefits of the project in measurable terms. This means that you must describe what it is you want to do in specific and detailed "outcome" statements. If at all possible, these outcome statements should be expressed in measurable terms. The objectives may describe the outcomes in terms of changes in behavior, new processes to be developed, or new products applied. In some cases they

Figure 8. Sample Proposal Introduction

Since its foundation in 1935, the Washington State Department of Game (DOG) has been charged with the management of sports fish and all of Washington's wildlife. The DOG is divided into six regions to provide public service throughout the state. Along with wildlife management of animals that are hunted, the department also provides programs for non-game animals and endangered species. DOG manages and protects all of the wildlife in the state for all of the citizens of Washington, for the purposes of recreation, aesthetic beauty and sound ecology, and for the benefit of future generations.

The DOG provides a wide variety of programs throughout the state as well as managing public lands for diverse recreational activities. The department sponsors educational talks with school groups about wildlife, hunter safety education programs, advice to private land owners on wildlife management, wildlife surveys and studies, game farms, and fish hatcheries. It also works with other public agencies such as the U.S. Forest Service, Inner Agency Council for Recreation, Department of Ecology, Department of Natural Resources, and others including public interest groups.

The DOG provides services to all citizens in the State of Washington whether or not the individual is a hunter or a fisherman. The primary source of funding for the department is the sale of licenses and tags. Some monies are received from the federal government for specific programs, and the department has received grants from the Kessler Corporation, Texaco, Friends of Wildlife, and others. "The Department of Game", states the Kessler Corporation, "effectively manages the rich and diverse wildlife populations of the state for all to enjoy, including educating the public to better appreciate their natural resources."

The DOG has already established two environmental education/visitor centers in western Washington at Marshy Creek in Olympia and Ariohead on the San Juan Islands. The purpose of this project is to construct a similar center in the southeastern part of the state, the Yakima region. The center would be constructed at the Oak Creek Wildlife Habitat Management Area where thousands of people come annually to view wintering elk and bighorn sheep.

may be expressed in terms of levels of performance called performance objectives. To be successful at this task, objectives should describe the outcomes or end products to be attained, the time period in which the expectations will be achieved, the conditions under which action will occur, and, if possible, how much will occur. Using action verbs that indicate measurable outcomes will help in this process: "To increase", "to reduce", or "to decrease" are objective action type statements. "To provide", "to create", or "to develop" are procedural type statements, not outcome statements. Procedures are a part of methods and will be covered in that section.

This performance or outcome statement includes each of the key elements described.

Over the first six months of the grant process, Operation Lifeline will increase by 10% its defined outreach services to elderly who are at the poverty level.

This example explains who is going to do what, when it will be accomplished, how it will be accomplished, and by what standard the accomplishment will be evaluated. The more specific the objective, the better.

It is important that at least one outcome statement or objective for each problem/need be identified in the need statement. This means that there will be one or more outcome statements in the objectives section for each of the problems/needs listed in the need statement, and at least one activity listed in the methods section for each outcome statement presented in the objectives section. Each section of the proposal narrative leads logically into the next, giving the proposal consistency. An example of a proposal objectives section is provided in Sample 7.

Figure 9. Sample Needs Statement

Many elderly people suffer the multiple threats of chronic disability, poverty, social isolation, and reduced mobility. It becomes increasingly more difficult for them to maintain an independent lifestyle since they feel vulnerable to medical and environmental emergencies and are often living alone and "out of reach." Thus, many older adults are confronted with limited health care options that may include 1. institutionalization; 2. securing daily home health care services through local agencies or homemaker help from relatives and friends; and/or 3. living with their unsatisfactory situations.

The costs and availability of institutions and service options are obviously a limiting factor; limiting in the sense that institutional care may not be affordable or desirable to elderly. Further, home health services are generally not adequate to meet the constant demand. Based on 1990 Census Data, 16.7 percent, or 28,913 residents of Portage County's population are aged 60 or older. Of this total, 24 percent or 7,046 elderly persons live alone, and 35 percent of these people who live alone have incomes below the poverty level. In addition, 5,723 people are disabled to the extent that they are prevented from working. Both the elderly and the disabled share the jeopardy of living alone on a fixed income with chronic health problems in relative isolation.

Portage County demonstrates a definite need to assist these elderly and disabled residents who are not capable of maintaining an independent living situation. This assistance should be such that the individual's personal security and self worth are maintained. The Operation Lifeline Program has been established to meet these needs.

Methods

The methods section describes in as much detail as necessary the activities to be accomplished in the project. This section describes how the project objectives will be accomplished. It should consider the following items:

- The overall design of the project.

- Specific activities that are planned.

- The relationship between activities and objectives.

- The specific procedures used to implement the program.

- How program participants will be selected.

- The personnel, facilities, and equipment that will be needed.

- The role key personnel will play, including program participants.

- The time schedule or timelines indicating completion of project components.

- Who will administer the project.

- Plans for cooperative arrangements with support agencies.

- Description of project "deliverables," e.g. newsletters, training materials, publications, treatment procedures, patents or copyrights, seminars or workshops, and project reports.

Figure 10. Sample Project Objectives

The primary objectives of the Operation Lifeline Program are:

1. To help the low income elderly and/or disabled maintain independence in their own homes with the greatest possible security, confidence, and dignity by the addition of 30 new Lifeline Units in 1997.

2. To reduce the sense of isolation for the elderly and/or disabled and to provide a feeling of security that one can receive help quickly in case of accident or illness by conducting in-home demonstrations to train the subscriber about usage of the Lifeline System.

3. To decrease the threat of institutionalization and increase the opportunity to link frail persons at home with the full range of medical and social services available by adding a program coordinator to assure successful program operation.

4. To assure those that are socially isolated that they can receive protective emergency services in the case of crime or environmental stress, by providing ongoing Operation Lifeline procedural information through workshops/training seminars to all law enforcement agencies in Portage County.

5. To increase the ability to identify needy and other qualified subscribers within the community that could benefit from the Lifeline System, by continuous contact with all appropriate health services involved in providing subscriber referrals.

6. To maintain the quality of service Lifeline subscribers now enjoy as the quantity of Lifeline units increases by monitoring/analyzing documented reports provided by the SEMC Emergency Department to assure a long-term individual case management approach.

In your discussion related to project personnel it is necessary to consider the following guidelines:

- Include at least a one paragraph description of each of the key project personnel.

- Provide some type of experience or background information directly related to the project for each of the key personnel.

- It is not uncommon to place a full vita or resume for each of the key personnel in the proposal appendix.

- If project personnel will need to be hired after the project is awarded, provide job specifications and qualifications for each position to be hired. Detailed specifications should also be placed in the proposal appendix.

- Describe the use of all project consultants.

It is important that the methods section flow naturally from the project needs and objectives. It is not necessary that this section be extremely long or detailed; rather, it should cover all procedural bases in an organized and direct manner. It should describe a reasonable array of project activities that will be accomplished in a timely, organized fashion. Examples of a methods section are presented in the completed sample proposals listed in the Appendix.

Evaluation

Most external sources will ask for an evaluation section in your proposal. Evaluation is a process of posing value questions and collecting information of importance in the decision-making process in your project. There are several types of evaluation techniques that may be used in accomplishing this task. A short review of the most common types of evaluation will be helpful in understanding the process and organization of your evaluation plan.

Product Evaluation. An evaluation of the results of the program. It may also be called an outcome evaluation or a summative evaluation. The successful product evaluation determines the extent to which the program has achieved its stated objectives and the extent to which the accomplishments of objectives can be attributed to the program.

Process Evaluation. An evaluation of the conduct of the program. It may also be called a formative evaluation. This type of evaluation determines whether the program has been conducted in a manner consistent with stated objectives and examines the relationship of different program activities to overall program effectiveness.

External Evaluation. An evaluation conducted by an individual(s) who is not a part of your project staff, thus providing for an objective outside review.

Internal Evaluation. An evaluation conducted by a member(s) of the project staff thus providing for an inside review.

The decision as to which type(s) of evaluation is best for your project will likely depend on the resources available and the guidelines of both the funding source and the submitting agency. Whatever is decided, the main consideration should be the development of meaningful information that will benefit the project and those it is designed to serve.

Some characteristics of a good evaluation plan include the following:

- It clearly states the criteria of success.

- It addresses the major decisions that must be made.

- It is cost effective.

- It is manageable.

- It identifies any instruments or questionnaires to be used.

- It identifies any reports that will be produced.

- The basic design is appropriate for the project.

Since the evaluation section of a proposal will vary greatly according to project objectives, it is difficult to provide a single example of an evaluation plan. Sometimes application formats include the evaluation section as a part of the methods section. Examples of sample evaluation plans are presented in the sample grants in the Appendix.

Budget Preparation

External sources will always ask for a detailed budget with your proposal. Typically, government agencies require a great deal of detail and usually provide a budget form with instructions as a part of the application packet. Foundations and corporations, on the other hand, usually are less formal in their budget approach. It is always important, however, to present a well-thought-out and complete budget to any external source.

The budget delineates the costs to be requested from the funding source as well as those to be provided (either through agency match or by donation) from the submitting agency or other supporters. If the funding source provides a budget format to be followed, then by all means follow that format. If a format is not provided (and this is often the case) it is important that each of the main areas of the budget be covered in your budget presentation. In most cases it is also to your benefit to present a line item budget and a supporting budget narrative as a part of the overall budget presentation.

The following guidelines will be helpful as you begin to develop your project budget.

- Fill out all forms according to the instructions given.

- Estimate all costs very carefully and remember that they are estimates that will probably be adjusted when the actual award is given.

- Identify the total cost (project cost), the funding source cost (funds requested), and the submitting agency costs (donated or matching funds) for each line item.

- Inflation factors should be built into each budget line item.

- Make budget figures reasonable but as generous as the funding source guidelines provide.

- Include indirect costs that will pertain to the project.

- Identify and meet the cost sharing and/or matching fund expectations of the external source.

- Double check the consistency between the budget and the narrative portion of the proposal.

- Do not ask for budget items that the funding source state they will not support.

Line Item Budget

Each line item budget should cover at least three main categories: direct costs, which are further divided into personnel costs and non-personnel costs; and indirect costs. For those sources that will provide support for the development and construction of new areas and facilities, a fourth area entitled capital cost should be added. The development of a budget should identify each line item with a column for funds requested (from the external source), funds donated or matched (from the submitting agency), and total project funds (funds requested plus funds donated or matched equal total project funds). Personnel costs should include all salaries, wages, and fringe benefits (mandated, voluntary, and FICA) for all key project personnel. Non-personnel costs should include all program-related costs, such as: space costs and rentals; equipment costs; leases; consumable supplies including paper, pencils, letterhead, envelopes, and so on; travel, both in-state and out-of-state, directly related to project objectives; telephone, including installation fees and monthly rates; postage; printing; insurance; and all other contractual type of services.

Indirect costs are those costs incurred by the submitting agency for program administration that the funding source is willing to support. These indirect costs are usually a negotiated percentage of the total direct cost of the project. Some external funding sources will not pay indirect costs; others do it as a matter of routine. Indirect costs may vary from 0% to 50% of the direct cost.

Your budget presentation should show that you are going to use the awarded resources wisely. Most external sources want to provide support for program activity components rather than personnel costs. A general principle to follow in developing your budget is to keep a 40%:60% ratio, or better, between personnel and program activity expenditures. This means that in the great majority of cases, budgets should be weighted in the direction of program activity support.

The following are some points to consider as your budget is developed.

1. Under personnel costs, list each person to be employed by the project under separate line items. Identify the percentage of time spent in the project for each individual, showing the corresponding salary and fringe benefits.

2. Identify the percentage of each person's time that will be funded by the funding source and the percentage funded by the submitting agency. This time is usually expressed in FTE, full-time equivalent. A 1.0 FTE or 100% means full-time, while .25 FTE or 25% would mean a one-fourth part-time appointment. If voluntary time is given, you may count that as time funded by the submitting agency as long as the amount credited is consistent with the level of work performed. If it is uncertain what the salary level for a position should be, or if the volunteer is not specifically trained to perform the job function, minimum wage should be used for the salary.

3. It is important that all fringe benefit costs are covered for all personnel listed. Be very careful to identify the fringe benefit percentage for each personnel classification because professional staff and classified staff often have different benefit package percentages.

4. In most cases the fringe benefit costs are part of the total funding request so they must be figured as accurately as possible. In rare cases, some external sources *do not* include fringe benefits as part of the direct costs.

5. Consultants are usually considered part of non-personnel (program) costs because they are part of program evaluation and are generally hired on a contractual basis. Such contracts usually represent a substantial cost savings to the project because fringe benefits are not required. If consultant services are not contracted but rather considered

as part of personnel costs, then consultants must be identified in the personnel section and fringe benefits must be provided.

6. In non-personnel or program costs, if the submitting agency is supplying office space, desks, equipment, and so on as part of the project agreement, the fair market value of each of these items can and should be listed on the budget as part of the submitting agency match or donation support.

Many external sources will allow a variety of support services to be included as part of the submitting agency's match.

7. Unless specifically stated in the instructions, most external sources will not support the purchase of equipment and supplies that would typically be provided by the submitting agency as part of normal business operations. An exception to this would be the necessity of equipment or materials

Figure 11. Sample Budget

Project EXETRA I

Budget 1995-96

Category	Non-Federal Inst. Support	BEH/DPP Requested	Project Total
A. *Personnel*			
A-1 Project Director (.25 FTE, 12 mos.) or (25% for 12 mos.)	$18,085 (9 mos.)	$4,000 (3 mos.)	$22,085
A-2 Project Coordinator (1.0 FTE, 11 mos.)	—	17,778	17,778
A-3 Project Practicum Supervisor (1.0 FTE, 9 mos.)	—	15,000	15,000
A-4 Faculty Advisors to Project (3 @ .10 FTE, 9 mos.)	6,600	—	6,600
A-5 Project Secretary (Secretary II level, 12 mos. @ $800/mo.)	—	9,600	9,600
A-6 Project Trainees (4 @ GTF III, 30 FTE, 9 mos.)	—	17,200	17,200
A-7 College Work Study	—	750	750
TOTAL PERSONNEL	24, 685	64, 328	89,013
B. *Fringe Benefits*			
B-8 Standard 26%	6,418	12,058	18,476
B-9 Students 5%	—	860	860
B-10 College Work Study Personnel	—	188	188
C. *Travel*			
C-11 In-state			
C-12 Out-of-State	—	2,500	2,500
D. *Equipment*			
D-13 File cabinets, desks, chairs, etc.	1,000	—	1,000
D-14 Equipment maintenance contract	500	650	1,150

that are not normally accessible to the submitting agency.

8. It is difficult to obtain travel funds from external sources unless that travel has a direct impact on project success. Even in these cases, it is essential to provide a detailed justification for travel funds in the budget proposal.

9. The percentage of indirect costs should be clearly identified as a part of the budget. In some cases this percentage will be negotiated with the external funding source before your application is submitted. In other cases, the submitting agency routinely takes an established percentage of the total direct cost to support their activities and agency overhead. It is not uncommon for submitting agencies to take 50% or more of direct cost for indirect cost. It is important to find out very early whether the total amount of funds for which you apply will include the indirect costs. If indirect costs are required you must then reduce the direct costs enough to cover these indirect costs. This may

Project EXETRA I
Budget 1995-96
Page 2

Category	Non-Federal Inst. Support	BEH/DPP Requested	Project Total
E. *Supplies*			
E-15 Office and Classroom	$500	$650	$1,150
F. *Contractual*			
F-16 Photocopying (12 mos. @ $63)	200	556	756
G. *Consultants*			
G-17 Consultant: Contracting for Project Evaluation & Selected Course Instruction (1 class @ $1200 - 10 days @ $100/day)	—	2,200	2,200
H. *Other*			
H-18 Conference Registration Fees	—	300	300
H-19 Communications (Postage, Telephones)	250	1,200	1,450
H-20 Printing (Annual Report, Newsletter, Evaluation Materials)	—	1,200	1,200
H-21 Tuition GTF (520 X 3 X 4)	—	6,240	6,240
H-22 Tuition Program Fellow (520 X 12 X 4)	24,960	—	24,960
I. *Total Direct*			
I-23 Direct Cost	58,913	94,530	153,443
J. *Indirect*			
J-24 U. of O. 31.3% of TDC	18,440	—	18,440
J-25 31.3% less Fed. amt. allowed	22,525	—	22,525
J-26 Fed. (8% of Direct Charge)	—	7,063	7,063
TOTAL INDIRECT	40,965	7,063	48,028
K. *Total*			
K-27 Total Direct and Indirect Charges	$99,878	$101,593	$201,471

Figure 12. Sample Budget Narrative/Addendum

BUDGET ADDENDUM
Category Line Item Explanation
Project EXETRA I

A. Personnel:*

A-1** *Project Director*
The project director for Project EXETRA is S. Harold Smith. Dr. Smith has a 25 year history of service, practice, and teaching in therapeutic recreation. For the past three years, Dr. Smith has been the Project Coordinator (Director of Project EXTENDED). He will carry responsibility as the therapeutic recreation curriculum coordinator in the Department of Recreation and Park Management as well as Director of the Center of Leisure Studies. He will also be responsible for the overall administration of Project EXETRA. Dr. Smith will be appointed on state funds for the normal academic year and on Project EXETRA funds during the summer term. Summer term responsibilities will include administration and evaluation of the Project. (Vita information on Dr. Smith is in Appendix I, p. XXX).

A-2 *Project Coordinator*
The project coordinator position will be filled with notification of grant award and after a national search. Job qualifications for this position are found on page 38 of this text. The project coordinator will be responsible for day-to-day administration of the project as well as development and evaluation of the Doctoral phase of the project. In addition, this person will teach a minimum of 5 classes during the academic year. This person will be on full appointment during the academic year and half appointment during summer session all funded by Project EXETRA.

A-3 *Project Practice Supervisor*
The project practice supervisor will be filled upon notification of grant award and after a national search. Qualifications for this position will be found on Page 38 of this text. The practice supervisor will have responsibility over development and evaluation of the Master's phase of the project as well as selection and coordination of practical sites. In addition, this person will teach a minimum of four classes, including practicum supervision, during the academic year. This position will be funded by the project for the academic year only.

A-4 *Faculty Advisor*
This budget item represents the principle faculty member among those selected to be members of the Project Advisory Council. These individuals will be selected from the Department of Recreation and Park Management and the Center on Human Development. Other advisory council members will be selected from resources outside of the University of Oregon. Their financial contribution is *not* included within this budget item.

A-5 *Project Secretary*
The secretary designation is a basic secretarial position established on a full-time basis to handle correspondence, newsletters, annual reports, and other publications as well as to maintain the office for student advice and counseling. Responsibility for preparation of teaching materials related to the Project and the management of a specialized library maintained by the project also fall within this position. The position is housed within the Center of Leisure Studies, Department of Recreation and Park Management and is considered instrumental in assisting with accomplishing a majority of the project's objectives. All telephone calls, filing, correspondence, photocopying, proposal preparation, project reports, etc. are handled through the secretarial position.

---

*Headings refer to OE Form 9047, Section A. Budget Categories.
**Line items from supplementary budget statement on pages 5–6.

continued from page 42

A-6   *Project Trainees*
The project trainees are four Doctoral level individuals hired at the GTF III level to assist in forwarding the goals of the project. Each trainee is provided tuition and a stipend through the project. The trainees play vital roles as Project Team leaders, practicum supervisors and evaluation assistants. Appointments will be on a 9 month academic year basis. The project trainees will also teach one course per year. The project trainee idea was developed on a trial basis two years ago in Project EXTENDED. Their presence and input has been so successful that they are considered key to the success of Project EXETRA.

B. *Fringe Benefits*

B-8   These items support the fringe benefit package offered through the University of Oregon for full
B-9   time faculty and student employees as listed. Included within this package are FICA, retirement,
B-10   health and dental insurance, workmen's compensation, unemployment insurance and employee liability insurance. Exact amounts of each package depend on employee options and rate changes. The two percentages are based upon the University Business Office projection for 1995-96.

C. *Travel*

C-12   Project travel is based upon needs in two or three areas. First is travel to meetings And requested/required of BEH for project staff generally held in Washington, D.C. or national convention sites. Second is travel to national and regional meetings/conventions in which project personnel would be involved. Third is in-state travel to state conferences, meetings and in-service/consultation/practicum sited. A majority of our best practicum sites are an hour or more away from Eugene, thus necessitating practicum supervision funds. Additional involvement of EXETRA staff other than the project director is desired, therefore sufficient funds for two individuals are budgeted to select conferences. Funds have also been identified for at least one staff member to attend a Type I Evaluation workshop.

D. *Equipment*

D-13   The University of Oregon, while having limited support funds, has supplied office space to house project staff and the capital equipment necessary to carry out the project goals and objectives. Staff office space is provided within the main Recreation and Park Management office. GTF office space is available in another building managed by the department. All of the funds necessary for office upkeep are provided by the university.

D-14   A number of office machines, including a Power MacIntosh G3 computer, are available for full use of the project. The only stipulation of use upon receipt of this equipment has been the assurance to pay the regular maintenance agreements.

E. *Supplies*

E-15   As previously discussed, the College of HPERDG and the RPM Department will provide Project EXETRA with office space, desks, filing cabinets, and approximately $500 worth of office supplies. The remaining expenses for necessary supplies will be made up from project funds. Most of these supplies are over and above the classroom materials generally covered out of the department budget.

F. *Contractual*

F-16   This item covers the cost of the photocopying services needed in relation to the project. This budget category has proven invaluable in assisting with dissemination of numerous reports and descriptive materials related to previous grant materials.

continued from page 43

G. *Consultants*

G-17 This category is presented for two main reasons. First, as a resource to bring in an outside consultant to help evaluate the progress of the project. Second, even though the University of Oregon offers an outstanding array of academic and professional talent, it is desirable for selected experts in the area of therapeutic recreation to be brought to our campus to provide our students with some breadth of experiences.

H. *Other*

H-18 Registration fees for conferences are rapidly increasing. The University of Oregon requires these funds to be budgeted under an individual category title.

H-19 Communications and mailing items include payment for the updating of the office telephone system. A mailing of project promotional materials, publications and evaluation materials is also covered here. This item specifically meets the stated objectives concerning dissemination of project information and evaluation data.

H-20 Included within this category are printing of the project information flyers, application materials, newsletters, annual reports, and evaluation surveys and results.

H-21 The four doctoral level individuals hired at the GTF III position will have their tuition paid. This line item represents the tuition for academic appointments of three quarters.

H-22 *Project Fellows*
This line item represents twelve tuition waiver fellowships provided by the University of Oregon for masters degree students in Project EXETRA. Tuition waiver is provided for a minimum of three and a maximum of four quarters depending upon availability of funds. This item represents a unique cooperative effort between Project EXETRA and the University of Oregon that will be made possible only upon acceptance of this proposal by BEH. It should also be understood that this item shows the strong support that the University of Oregon is willing to provide to Project EXETRA.

I. *Total Direct Charges*

I-23 The figure of $58,913 represents the non-Federal, University of Oregon support for Project EXETRA. This is to complement the requested $94,530 of support from BEH/DPP. Total direct charges for Project EXETRA amount to $153,443.

J. *Indirect*

J-24/ The figure of $40,965 reflects 31.3% of the BEH/DPP and non-Federal institution direct costs
J-25 as allocated to the University of Oregon under Federal regulations.

J-26 The amount of eight percent of direct charges has been standard in previous grant applications from the Department of Recreation and Park Management and is consistent with Federal rules and regulations in this area.

K. *Total*

K-27 Total direct and indirect charges for Project EXETRA.

mean that you have to go back and adjust your program activities accordingly. For example, if you were applying for a $75,000 grant and you know that there will be a 20% indirect cost expectation, then your direct costs can total only $60,000 (20% of $75,000 = $15,000; $75,000 - $15,000 = $60,000).

An example of a line item budget is found in Figure 5. A review of this sample budget shows the submitting agency providing $99,878 in total direct and indirect costs, the external funding source being requested to provide $101,593 total direct and indirect costs, giving a total project cost of $201,471. The amount of detail needed in the line item budget will depend completely on the extensiveness of the project proposal.

Budget Narrative/Addendum

It is often a good practice to provide the funding source a budget narrative/addendum that gives a brief explanation of each of the budget lines. This budget narrative/addendum is usually attached to the project proposal in the proposal appendix. Figure 6 presents a budget narrative/addendum for the line item budget found in Figure 5. Additional examples of both line item budgets and budget narratives/addenda are found in the project proposals presented in the Appendix.

Appendix

The proposal appendix that comes at the end of the project proposal and may or may not be requested as part of your application procedures.

The appendix provides the opportunity to add support information and materials to your proposal that were prohibited by space or context in the proposal narrative. Appendix materials offer additional support, clarity, and credibility to your proposal. The appendix is divided into sections according to topic area and is identified on the table of contents. For an example of an appendix section, please review the appendix section of this book.

The type of materials that are generally presented in the appendix are:

1. review of related literature;

2. agency brochures, newsletters, year-end reports, and financial statements;

3. statistical data or studies that lend support and credibility to the proposal;

4. letters of support from key individuals and cooperating agencies;

5. budget narrative/addendum;

6. vitae of key project personnel;

7. listing of project job specifications;

8. samples of tests, questionnaires, or other evaluation materials;

9. samples of lesson plans, training materials, or similar deliverables;

10. detailed timelines for project implementation and evaluation;

11. any other item that you feel would be meaningful to the reviewer in support of your proposal.

Chapter Summary

Upon completion of your first draft, go back and summarize what you have written. This is done by asking yourself questions similar to those to be asked by the review panel. Provide the same questions to your colleagues and ask them to review the proposal. The questions below provide a summary checklist of those items you should have addressed before your proposal is ready for actual submission.

1. Has the rationale been stated clearly and convincingly? Does the submitting agency indicate an awareness of the problem? Is the proposal parochial or naive?

2. Have the objectives been specified operationally and in sufficient detail? Are they feasible? To what extent can the program be expected to accomplish the objectives? Do they claim too much? Are they trying to oversell? Are they funded by pious, unrealistic hopes?

3. What is the relationship of this proposal to other efforts in this particular area? Is the problem of enough significance to be worthy of funding? Who is most affected by the problem? How does the proposal fit into the submitting agency and the funding source philosophy and priorities?

4. Does the proposal suggest sound administrative practices? Does the submitting agency have a history of proper administrative procedures? Does the submitting agency have the capability of taking on a project of this magnitude?

5. Are salaries and personnel assignments appropriate? Are lines of authority identified appropriately? Does the proposal show fiscal accountability? To whom is the project accountable: consumers, general public, agency board?

6. Is the budget realistic? Is it enough to do the job? Is there sufficient slack to provide staff the flexibility to respond to emerging contingencies? Has the budget been padded?

7. Should this proposal have been submitted to this funding source? Does it fit better with some other agency? Should it have been submitted to a local giver?

8. Does the proposal meet the technical guidelines and regulations published for this type of proposal?

9. Can the project be effectively evaluated? Are project staff capable of performing the evaluation or will an external evaluator be needed? On what criteria will the project be evaluated?

10. Is the proposal well organized with completed application forms, proposal narrative, and budget detail indicating project consistency and strength?

The final question to ask is, **"What do I need to rewrite/revise to make my proposal more competitive?"**

Chapter 5

Steps Four, Five and Six:

Proposal Submission

Proposal Acceptance or Rejection

Project Management

Introduction

Your project proposal should now be to the point of submission consideration. As a final check, many application formats provide a checklist to follow so that all required information is submitted properly. In addition to this procedural checklist, it is often a good practice to review your total proposal one last time to see if all of the standards of a good proposal have been met. If a team has worked on the proposal or if you are working with an outside agency, it may be appropriate for all of those involved to sit down and work through the final draft together. The following are guidelines for a good completed proposal.

- The need for the proposed activity is clearly established and supported with meaningful data.

- The most important ideas are highlighted and repeated in several places.

- The project objectives are given in detail.

- There is a detailed schedule of project activities.

- Collaboration with all interested groups is evident throughout the proposal.

- The commitment of all involved groups is evident through letters of support, cost sharing, and so on.

- The proposal narrative, budget detail, and budget narrative all tell the same story.

- Fund allocation is clearly indicated in the proposal narrative and in the budget detail.

- All of the major requirements listed in the application instructions are clearly addressed.

- The agreement of all project staff, consultants, and collaborating groups is clearly indicated.

- All government procedures have been followed with regard to such areas as civil rights compliance and protection of human subjects.

- Appropriate detail is provided in all sections of the proposal.

- Appendices have been used wisely to provide additional support materials.

- The length is consistent with expectations of the external source.

- The budget detail is clear and accurate.

- The qualifications of the submitting agency and its staff are clearly communicated.

As you review these standards, you may need to revise parts of the proposal one last time. Don't be afraid to do revisions as often as you feel it will be to your benefit. Also recognize, however, that timelines must be met and in some cases you must do the best you can with time and resources available.

Proposal Submission

Once the proposal is written, revised and ready to submit, many proposal writers feel their task is complete. NOT SO! Following the submission directions to the last detail is the next important step. Some considerations that you must give to the submission process follow.

- How many copies of the proposal are to be submitted? Many external sources want the original plus three to seven copies.

- What is the submission deadline? Submission deadlines ARE NOT flexible. Most instructions will note whether the application packet must arrive by a certain date or just be postmarked by a certain date. Many post offices do not

automatically postmark all of their mail. This may mean that you will need to go to your local post office and see that your application packet is post-marked correctly.

- Many submitting agencies have their own internal approval process that may take up to a week to complete. If you don't know this process ahead of time, you may not be able to obtain the necessary approvals and signatures before the submission deadline.

- With many government RFAs/RFPs several notification forms and/or post-cards are required with the application submission. If these forms are not sent, your application will not be reviewed.

- If timelines get very close, remember that many locations have access to one day or overnight postal and/or delivery service.

In most cases, the funding source will notify you of receipt of your application materials. This source will also give you a tentative date by which you can expect a decision. Be aware that the funding source may accept all or only a part of your total proposal. In most cases the contact officer for the funding source will respond to you and negotiate the exact project activities and budget items they are willing to support.

Submission to Multiple Agencies

Because of the high mortality rate of proposal submissions, it is not uncommon for submitting agencies to submit all or part of a proposal to more than one funding source for considera-tion. If this is done, it is a matter of courtesy to inform each of your actions. At best, it is in poor taste — and at worst illegal — to accept an award for the same project from more than one source. Certainly, it raises some very delicate ethical questions that must be addressed. If your pro-posal should receive more than one positive response, careful negotiations with all involved parties are indicated to insure that no one is offended and that support is not lost. This is, of course, one of the pleasant problems in gaining a project award!

Proposal Acceptance or Rejection

If your grant application is rejected, **don't give up** and **do not take it personally**. Remember that the first award is the most difficult to obtain. To help with future applications, ask the funding source to explain why your proposal was rejected. Most are willing to provide this information to you. Use this information to revise your proposal and make it stronger. Submit it again in the next com-petitive round or locate another potential source and give them a try. In some cases, a proposal will need to be submitted two or three times before an award is received.

Project Administration

When you do receive a project award, realize that you have been successful in only the first phase of the project award process. The second phase is the effective management of your project so that project objectives and activities are accom-plished in a positive manner. If you do not manage your award effectively, it is less likely that you will receive additional support from the external source. If, however, you do a good job in project administration, you are almost guaranteed addi-tional award support in the future, if funds are available.

Some easy to follow but often overlooked suggestions for effective project management follow.

- Whenever possible, select only one person to be your contact with the external source.

- If you have questions about your proposal, contact the contact officer with the funding source for clarification.

- Send correspondence to a person, usually the contact officer, not just an address.

- When signing documents, always include the date and title of the person signing. Do not take responsibility in areas where you have no official jurisdiction.

- When submitting a continuation proposal, resubmit all required materials rather than referring to materials already on file.

- vInclude your project name and grant identification number on all correspondence.

- Be as direct and specific as possible in all correspondence.

- Send separate letters for each project in question when several different proposals may be involved.

- Always ask before making any changes in the budget.

- Keep multiple projects in separate files and administer them separately. This is especially important with budgetary items.

- Keep your funding source well informed of project progress and accomplishments. Periodically write a letter or call to provide them with project updates. Always send them copies of project newsletters, year-end reports, etc.

- Actively direct your project to a prompt and satisfactory completion.

- At the completion of your project, complete and submit all required reports and statements in a timely and professional manner.

Chapter Summary

Finally, it would be beneficial to consider the following common reasons that most proposals are rejected.

1. *The applicant did not follow the guidelines provided by the external source.*

- The application did not provide all of the information requested.

- The proposal objectives did not match the objectives of the external source.

- The proposal budget was not in the range of the funding identified by the external source.

- Local matching funds or resources were inadequate or uncertain.

2. *The proposal application lacked credibility.*

- Key phrases or target populations were not identified or were repeated so often that they became meaningless.

- The proposal depended on a "sympathetic" review panel to understand and accept poorly presented materials.

- The application had inflated rhetoric and assumed that the review panel was familiar with or predisposed to support the proposal.

- Prospective client groups were not involved in the planning and development of the objectives and activities.

- There was a lack of community support for the project.

- The proposal was poorly written, difficult to understand, and/or sloppily presented.

- There was a lack of evidence that the project would continue beyond the award period.

- The proposal had not been coordinated with other individuals and organizations working in the same area.

- The proposal objectives were too ambitious and/or the budget was unrealistic.

3. *Project activities were not adequately explained.*

- Problems had not been clearly documented.

- The identified problem did not appear significant enough for external award support.

- The needs, objectives, and program activities did not support each other.

- The budget did not accurately support program activities.

Chapter 6

Bond/Millage Campaigns

Introduction

City governments struggle to maximize shrinking budgets and at the same time try to meet the ever-expanding needs of the community. Assessing the public needs and seeking new ways to pay for these services is an ongoing challenge. As citizens demand more services, many cities and towns are looking at bond/millage issues to meet those demands. Bond issues are used as means to assist city recreation programs, e.g., community centers, ice skating rinks, water parks, swimming pool, and libraries, and to renovate or build new schools.

The foundation of a successful bond issue campaign is well laid out before public opinion polls, focus groups, or architectural renderings are presented. It is vital to establish task forces and involve community members of various ages, cultures, and backgrounds to participate in every phase of the campaign from concept to construction.

Pre-Campaign Feasibility Study

Through a series of confidential interviews with 40-50 selected representatives from key internal and external constituencies, an objective assessment is made of the potential to raise a suggested campaign goal associated with a defined program or project. The following elements should be considered during the study:

- Analysis of the case for perceived support by the donor community.

- Identification of candidates for possible volunteer leadership positions.

- Analysis of required gift pattern.

- Assessment of community leadership attitude regarding the role of the non-profit organization and its programming impact on the citizens in the community.

- Review of necessary pre-solicitation "education" and cultivation strategies.

- Estimate of available volunteerism for solicitation effort.

- Determination of best "timing" for campaign based on other current or proposed community campaigns.

- Review of necessary support systems and records management capabilities necessary for intensive campaign solicitation and follow-up.

The following schedule for a feasibility study is frequently followed:

1. *Two to Three Weeks* – development and approval of the case for support and interview list, preparation and distribution of letters requesting interview appointments;

2. *Six Weeks* – conduct of personal interviews;

3. *Two to Three Weeks* – compilation and analysis of data and preparation of study report. (Depending upon interviewing, this schedule might be compressed.)

In some funding projects it may be appropriate to attempt multiple fund raising activities, e.g., a $1.2 million capital campaign and a $1.8 million bond issue proposal.

Consultants may be used to help develop your case for support or to discourage your community from proceeding. Some issues that might deter the community include:

- Philanthropic competition in the community is high.

- Provision of future operating support is unclear.

- There is perceived duplication of services with other community institutions.

- There is a perception that computer and information technology will play a limited role.

- There is lack of understanding of the need for a new facility.

The feasibility study may review the following points:

Favorable Factors

- Community Pride

- The Site

- The Layout/Floor Plan

- Current Programs

Unfavorable Factors

- Concept

- Funding

- Competition

- Timing

The Feasibility Study should include possible recommendations such as:

- Establish a program committee to identify current and future programs, services, and resources that the community has/will require.

- Establish a steering committee to formulate and implement an effective awareness program. The initial purpose will be to raise awareness of the project and the campaign rather than to raise dollars.

- Create a building committee which will include members of the program committee to work with architects to plan and lay out site and facility.

- Create a campaign cabinet composed of members of the three above committees, as well as at-large members of the broader community including, but not limited to neighborhood groups, parent association members, other civic leaders, and parents of young children. This committee is to take responsibility for developing the campaign plan, policies, procedures, and budget.

The overall evaluation of the fund raising potential should be based upon the following assumptions:

- This project will include a grassroots style campaign focusing on small gifts from individual donors, community groups, and civic organizations, as well as on major gifts from individuals, businesses, and foundations.

- The completion of a successful campaign will provide the springboard for initiating a district-wide bond or millage to support the capital and operational needs for the new facility.

- The planning team will develop or plan to accommodate a "gifts in-kind" strategy and various memorial and commemorative opportunities. This campaign lends itself to a grassroots style of campaign which could include such solicitation strategies as "buy-a-brick" or "place your name in history."

Five Communication Tips to Gain Grassroots Community Support

1. Word-of-mouth is the best way to gain support. Information that causes people to adopt new ideas comes from other people they believe and trust.

2. Convince opinion leaders to support your cause and they will influence the majority of the community to follow. Build relationships and communicate with early adopters.

3. Do not expect impersonal communication or mass media to change people's behavior.

4. The best way to convince opinion leaders is by building relationships with them — Friend Raising. Create a program to identify opinion leaders and communicate with them on a regular basis
in an attempt to build long-term relationships.

5. Utilize employees to build relationships. Enlist the help of employees as they are already talking about your organization with family, friends, and people of influence in the community.

Committees and Tasks

Successful campaigns may also include some of the following committees or individuals in addition to the committees listed in the feasibility study:

Chairperson

- Chair the bond/millage committee meetings.

- Motivate volunteer committee members and help create interest in the community.

- Oversee campaign theme and plan.

- Select other chairs and find a treasurer.

- Thank the community, win or lose.

Finance Committee

- By statute, governmental agencies and schools cannot pay for bond/millage campaigns out of their own budgets.

- Determine a budget and seek the necessary funds.

- Register the campaign committee with the county clerk.

- Open a checking account and keep financial records.

- Close the books and file the necessary paperwork.

Public Relations/Marketing/Publicity Committee

- Develop a theme for your campaign, e.g., Bonding Together for Quality Recreation Services.

- Consider some of the following:

Print/Graphic

- User statistics – charts

- Millage pro forma – examples

- Newspaper feature stories

- Brochures

- Buttons, stickers, balloons

- Refrigerator magnets

- Bookmarks

- Ribbons, lapel pins

- Grocery bag imprints

- Bumper stickers

- POP displays in stores

- Store window posters

- Door hangers

- Press releases

- Reprints of favorable articles

- Direct mail

- Yard signs

- Signs on way to polls

- Newspaper inserts

- Stickers to place on calendars to remind them the day of the vote

- Postcards to "Yes" voters

- Church bulletin inserts

- Have letters to the editor ready when a negative one appears, particularly if misleading information is presented.

Person-to-Person

- Letters or cards to friends, neighbors
- Door-to-door visits
- Election-eve phone calls
- Telephone canvassing

Broadcast

- Develop a video
- Radio public service announcements (PSA) by community leaders
- Cable channel PSAs
- Radio interviews
- Radio call-in programs

Special Events

- Public tours of existing facilities
- Block parties, open houses, coffee klatches, receptions, etc.
- Community dialogs
- On-going press coverage
- Rallies
- Centrally located progress chart
- Letters to editor
- Endorsements by community leaders
- Letters to absentee voters
- Pledge cards
- Campaign among current 18 year olds

Yes Voters

- Identify the number of yes voters you think it will take to win the election
- Attempt to determine those people you think will vote yes, either by pledge cards or by calling people, and develop a data bank
- Call yes voters the night before the election
- On election day have poll watchers at the different precincts and, again, call the yes voters who have not voted

Speakers Bureau

- Develop a list of groups for presentations, e.g., service clubs, unions, parent groups, businesses, and industries
- Arm the speakers with facts and figures for their presentations

Other Brainstorming Ideas

- Market the good
- Stress quality
- Target market
- What it costs the taxpayer in dollars and cents (pennies), i.e., less than a cup of coffee per day
- Use simple terms
- What is your competition doing?
- Provide the actual nuts and bolts of what a positive vote will provide and what it will not

Millage/Bond Election Campaign Proposed Timeline

This is a ten (10) week campaign leading up to election day.

Week Ten

- Identify and recruit campaign leadership

- Work with election officials to schedule special election in each voting district

- Develop case for support

- Develop a campaign budget

- Identify funding sources

Week Nine

- Identify campaign volunteers for all voting districts

- Contact donor prospects to arrange meetings to solicit campaign funds

- Identify target voters and begin building database

- Develop promotional plan, including endorsements, media contacts and kick-off event, letters to the editor

- Begin developing campaign materials: brochures, fliers, lawn signs, etc.

Week Eight

- Begin recruiting campaign volunteers from all districts

- Continue soliciting funds

- Continue building database

- Organize speakers bureau, identify speakers and destinations

- Plan absentee voter efforts

- Continue working on campaign materials

- Begin acquiring endorsements from community business leaders

- Begin organizing block parties or similar campaign support events within all voting district(s)

Week Seven

- Continue recruiting campaign volunteers

- Continue soliciting funds

- Continue building database

- Begin scheduling speakers

- Finalize campaign materials

- Begin acquiring media endorsements

- Continue acquiring endorsements from community and business leaders

- Continue absentee voter efforts

- Initiate letter writing campaign

- Begin organizing phone bank

Week Six

- Prepare campaign packets for businesses and organizations

- Prepare mailing to friends and patrons

- Continue scheduling speakers

- Continue recruiting campaign volunteers

- Continue building database

- Continue acquiring endorsements

- Continue organizing telephone bank

- Prepare for campaign kick-off

- Continue absentee voter efforts

Week Five

- Conduct campaign kick-off

- Mail campaign packets to businesses and organizations

- Mail campaign materials to friends and patrons

- Distribute lawn signs and other promotional materials

- Continue acquiring endorsements

- Finalize plans for telephone bank

- Continue letter writing campaign

- Continue absentee voter efforts

Week Four

- Distribute promotional materials to businesses

- Initiate telephone campaign

- Continue acquiring endorsements

- Continue letter writing

Week Three

- Begin "block parties"/support events in the townships

- Continue absentee voter efforts

- Place media ads

- Secure media endorsements

- Begin door-to-door canvassing

- Mail literature to target voters

- Continue telephone bank activities

- Continue letter writing

Week Two

- Continue media ads

- Continue absentee voter efforts

- Use media endorsements

- Continue block parties/support activities

- Continue telephone bank activities

- Continue letter writing

Week One

- Continue absentee voter efforts

- Continue block parties/support events

- Continue telephone bank activities

- Continue letter writing

- Hand out campaign literature at designated spots

- Continue media ads

Election Day

- Arrange for transportation and babysitting, if needed

- Continue telephone bank activities

- Finish absentee voter efforts

- Perform poll greeting and watching activities

- VOTE!

- ***Hold victory party and celebrate!***

Day After Election Day

- Take down all the signs

- Begin the process of writing Thank You notes to the volunteers and committee chairs

- Thank the community for their support

- Close the books and register the group inactive until the next time

Chapter 7

Fund Raising and Development

Overview of Fund Raising and Development

Fund raising happens when a donor makes a contribution to your organization in exchange for a premium, product, or anything of value. A good example of this is selling Girl Scout cookies. In the State of Michigan in 1998 the Girl Scouts of America made $38 million in profit. Development on the other hand, is a process that includes the identification of constituents who are interested and committed to your organization and are willing to invest in its future. Development is getting people to invest in your future by committing to your mission.

In 1996 Americans contributed $135 billion to charities and in 1997 that figure rose to $143 billion. Eighty percent (80%) of that money given to charities comes from individuals, ten percent (10%) from bequests, six percent (6%) from foundations, and four percent (4%) from corporations. Almost half of the individual contributions are made to religious organizations. Americans in 1999 contributed a record $190 billion, a forty one percent (41%) increase since 1995. Seven in ten American homes made at least one charitable contribution in 1999 and even half of all Americans who make less than $10,000 made at least one charitable contribution. Successful fundraisers need to develop a relationship with individuals to gain access to the remaining half that they donate to other causes.

A totally integrated development plan starts with an assessment of the needs of the organization, a review of the mission, and the determination of short- and long-range programmatic goals. Once this is successfully completed you may begin an evaluation of funding sources that must be raised to support programs to resolve the needs, and the selection, of appropriate fund raising programs to raise the required funds. Fund raising programs are the annual fund, capital campaign, and planned giving (Appendix D).

The Annual Fund

Developing a comprehensive annual giving program should be a priority of all organizations. The basic purpose of the annual fund is to acquire new donors, renew existing donors, and upgrade the donation.

Purposes of the annual fund are:

- Establish habits and patterns of giving.

- Once the pattern is established it may lead to bigger capital gifts.

- A means of getting out the message about your organization on a yearly basis.

- To have the organization be accountable for its stewardship on an annual basis.

Preparing a Case/Needs Statement for Annual Giving

- What are the external needs that are reflected in your mission, e.g., new/expanded programs?

- What are your internal needs, e.g., equipment or technology?

- What is a reasonable goal for your campaign?

Preparing a Gift Range Chart and Setting Fund Raising Goals

- What quality (and how many) gifts are required?

- How many prospects are required to justify each level of the gift range chart?

- Must be challenging, yet realistic.

- Must be developed together and understood by all.

Fund Raising Organization

- Chart the fund raising organization you will use.

- Get your board to make annual personal gifts as an expression of commitment and to provide personal testimony to the value of the organization and the legitimacy of its needs.

Strategies for the Annual Fund

- Direct mail

- Phone appeals

- Personal solicitation

- Recognition groups

- Challenge gifts

- Grant proposals

- Special events

Successful Tips in a Direct Mail Campaign

- The more personal or "targeted" the better; will be more effective.

- For first time donors ask for a specific amount, e.g., $100. To those who have given before, ask for an increase in giving.

- If you say in your letter you will follow-up with a phone call, "do it", as only one in ten follow-up.

- Make it easy to respond.

- Promote pledging and spread out payments over the year.

- People give to people — get the right person to sign the letter.

- Don't forget the return envelope.

- Make your case clearly and directly.

- Keep it simple and inviting to give.

The Capital Campaign

- The capital campaign is an intensive fund raising program designed to raise a specific amount of money. It is usually used for the capital needs of the organization, such as building projects, remodeling, expansion, and equipment acquisition.

- The capital campaign usually requires large gifts that represent transfers from assets rather than gifts from income.

- A capital campaign allows the donor to pay over a number of years. This is called the "pledge" system of giving.

Considering a Capital Campaign: Are You Ready?

- The organization must have a positive image.

- The case for support must appeal to the interests and desires of your prospective contributors.

- There must be a high degree of understanding and acceptance of the program.

- As solicitors are volunteers, influential and interested leaders need to be a part of the campaign organization.

- The dollar objective should be attainable.

- Campaign timing should not conflict with other major fund raising programs.

- The inner group or campaign cabinet must be willing to lead, to work, and to give financially.

Tips for a Successful Capital Campaign

The total campaign budget should not exceed ten percent (10%) of the final campaign goal. A typical lead gift is ten percent (10%) to twelve percent (12%) of your overall goal; then work

your way down and build a pyramid. Make this gift table based on the feasibility study (see Appendix E and F).

- If building a facility, review the most popular rooms and match those areas with the gifts or level of gifts. This can be used with solicitation or in the acknowledgment phase. This is a powerful tool used in development.

- Allow for various levels of giving by all segments of your community, e.g., Buy a Brick is a lower giving level attainable by a large percentage of people.

- Choose your campaign cabinet carefully, including people of diverse backgrounds.

- Have fun in the process of fund raising.

- Develop a realistic time line recognizing seasonal realities and volunteers' time commitments.

- Recognize your donors with acknowledgment letters, names in newsletters/ newspapers, invitations to special organization events, recognition plaques and wall of fame. You cannot thank contributors enough.

Two Examples of Capital Campaigns

Community Playground

Goal $105,000

Sold Components –		
e.g., swings, bridges, parallel bars		$ 72,000
Pickets or fencing – names engraved in posts		11,000
Coins From Clouds – coins in yogurt cups		
in schools		5,500
Grants		18,000
Matching Dollars with hospital and doctors		22,000
	Total	$128,500

Community Library

Goal $1.2 million		Two lead gifts: $800,000	
Major Contributor	Goal: $100,000	Raised	$174,820
Foundation	Goal: $250,000	Raised	85,000
Families	Goal: $ 50,000	Raised	58,820
Business	Goal: $ 75,000	Raised	161,360
Community	Goal: $ 75,000	Raised	100,000
Buy a Brick			20,000
		Total	$1.4 million

Planned Giving

A planned gift program is a sophisticated fund raising plan that offers various gift-making alternatives to the prospective donor.

- The term "Planned Gifts" is increasingly used, replacing the old term "deferred gifts."

- A "planned gift " is legally provided for during the donor's lifetime, but principal benefits do not accrue until a future time, generally at the death of the donor and/ or the income beneficiary.

- A planned gift is given to your organization now, but is subject to certain contracted obligations. The gift is actually received by your organization when the terms and conditions of the contract are fulfilled.

- Planned giving connotes thoughtful preparation and planning, and can apply to all forms of gifts. The term is used most commonly for gifts of future interest.

There are a number of planned gift opportunities:

- Bequests: A donor leaves all or part of his/her estate in a will.

- Gifts of Life Insurance: Your organization is named as beneficiary on a life insurance policy.

- Loans and Deposit Agreements: A donor gives you money which you invest to earn income.

- Annuities/Trusts: A donor transfers assets to your organization. These you invest and pay the donor from those investments.

- Pooled Income Funds: Also known as charitable mutual funds, when multiple donors contribute assets which are invested and earnings are divided.

- Life Estate Contracts: A donor gives you a remainder interest in a personal residence, but retains an interest in this asset for life.

Funding Errors

Dr. Jeffrey L. Lant, president of his own management and development firm for non-profit organizations, writes about the twelve worst fund raising errors:

- Not targeting the right donors

- Not planning ahead

- Not involving your board

- Not finding links to corporations and foundations

- Not writing persuasive fund raising documents

- Not cultivating givers

- Not seeking large capital gifts

- Not keeping good fund raising records

- Not being persistent

- Not telling donors about your successes

- Not developing sources of local support

- Not sending out enough direct mail letters

Fund Raising and Development Guidelines That Never Age!

- People give to people and for people.

- The right person makes the difference in successful fund raising.

- The one who asks, must give first.

- See each prospect face-to-face.

- Ask for a specific amount, ask for enough.

- It may not be fun, but its crucial.

Appendix A

Sample RFAs/RFPs

Governmental – "Community Partners for
Healthy Farming *Intervention – CDC*"

Foundation – "The James S.
McDonnell Foundation"

Governmental

"COMMUNITY PARTNERS FOR HEALTHY FARMING INTERVENTION – CDC"

(*Federal Register*: February 10, 1999, Volume 64, Number 27)

Centers for Disease Control and Prevention (Program Announcement 99039)

Community Partners for Healthy Farming Intervention; Notice of Availability of Funds

A. Purpose

The Centers for Disease Control and Prevention (CDC) announces the availability of fiscal year (FY) 1999 funds for a cooperative agreement program for Community Partners for Healthy Farming. This program addresses the "Healthy People 2000" priority areas of Community-Based Programs and Occupational Safety and Health. The purpose of this cooperative agreement is to utilize the special resources of researchers, workers, farm managers, local agricultural communities, and other stakeholders to evaluate farm safety and health interventions.

B. Eligible Applicants

Applications may be submitted by public and private nonprofit and commercial organizations and by governments and their agencies; that is, universities, colleges, research institutions, hospitals, other public and private nonprofit and commercial organizations, state and local governments or their bona fide agents, and federally recognized Indian tribal governments, Indian tribes, or Indian tribal organizations.

Note: Public Law 104-65 states that an organization described in section 501(c)(4) of the Internal Revenue Code of 1986 that engages in lobbying activities is not eligible to receive federal funds constituting an award, grant, cooperative agreement, contract, loan, or any other form.

C. Availability of Funds

Approximately $850,000 is available in FY 1999 to fund five to seven awards. It is expected that the average award will be $145,000, ranging from $45,000 to $180,000. It is expected that the awards will begin on or about August 1, and will be made for a 12 month budget period within a project period of up to four years. Funding estimates may change. Continuation awards within an approved project period will be made on the basis of satisfactory progress as evidenced by required reports and the availability of funds.

D. Funding Preferences

Funding preferences may be given to applications from specific locations to achieve geographic distribution.

E. Cooperative Activities

In conducting activities to achieve the purpose of this program, the recipient will be responsible for activities under 1. (Recipient Activities), and CDC/NIOSH will be responsible for the activities listed under 2. (CDC/NIOSH Activities).

1. Recipient Activities

a. Developing an intervention with a clear prevention effect, evidence of community support and strategies for adoption by the community, and for sustainability.

b. Develop a research proposal which is predicated upon an active partnership between experienced researchers, communities, agricultural workers,

management and other stakeholders in the planning, implementation, and evaluation of intervention known agricultural injuries, illness, or hazards. The evaluation component shall include both process and outcome evaluation. The study population and recruitment procedures should be described. A time line which includes post intervention analyses should be developed.

c. Implement, collect and analyze the evaluation data.

d. Identify and implement measures to maintain and extend the intervention.

2. CDC/NIOSH Activities

a. Provide technical assistance, through site visits and other communication, in all phases of the development, implementation and maintenance of these cooperative agreements.

b. Facilitate communication/coordination between recipients and other groups, organizations and agencies involved in agricultural research and outreach.

c. Assist in the development of a research protocol for Institutional Review Board (IRB) review by all cooperating institutions participating in the research project.

The CDC IRB will review and approve the protocol initially and on at least an annual basis until the research project is completed.

F. Application Content

Use the information in the Cooperative Activities, Other Requirements, and Evaluation Criteria sections to develop the application content. Your application will be evaluated on the criteria listed, so it is important to follow them in laying out your program plan. The narrative should be no more than 50 double-spaced pages. The original and each copy of the application must be submitted unstapled and unbound. All materials must be typewritten, double-spaced, with unreduced type (font size 12 point) on 8 1/2" by 11" paper, with at least 1" margins, headers, and footers, and printed on one side only.

Do not include any spiral or bound materials or pamphlets. Appendices should have indices and include (1) support letters, (2) information on key personnel, (3) other supporting documentation.

G. Submission and Deadline

Letter of Intent (LOI)

The letter of intent must be submitted on or before March 23, to: Sheryl L. Heard, Grants Management Specialist, Grants Management Branch, Procurement and Grants Office, Announcement 99039, Centers for Disease Control and Prevention (CDC), 2920 Brandywine Road, Mail Stop E-13, Atlanta, Georgia 30341.

Application

Submit the original and two copies of PHS 5IL61-1 IOMB Number 0937-0189. Forms are in the application kit. On or before April 23, submit the application to: Sheryl Heard, Grants Management Specialist. Grants Management Branch, Procurement and Grants Office, Announcement 99039, Centers for Disease Control and Prevention (CDC), 2920 Brandywine Road, Mail Stop E-13, Atlanta, Georgia 30341.

Deadline

Applications shall be considered as meeting the deadline if they are either:

1. Received on or before the deadline date; or

2. Sent on or before the deadline date and received in time for orderly processing. (Applicants must request a legibly dated U.S. Postal Service postmark or obtain a legibly dated receipt from a commercial carrier or U.S. Postal Service. Private metered postmarks shall not be acceptable as proof of timely mailing).

   Late Applications: Applications which do not meet the criteria in (a) or (b) above are considered late applications, will not be considered, and will be returned to the applicant.

H. Evaluation Criteria

Applications which are complete and responsive will be reviewed and evaluated by an Independent Special Emphasis Panel in accordance with the following criteria.

1. Background and Need (20 points total)

   a. The extent to which the applicant understands the purpose and provides a comprehensive statement of the specific problem to be addressed (12 points).

   b. The extent to which the applicant presents data justifying the need for the intervention in terms of magnitude of the problem and the intervention is theoretically justified and supported with epidemiological, methodological, or behavioral research (9 points).

   c. The extent to which the intervention is feasible and can be expected to produce the expected results in the target group. Efficacy of adoption and sustainability of the intervention acknowledging potential strengths and barriers to adoption and sustainability, e.g., the impact of trends in agriculture, support by partners and stakeholders, costs of implementation, effects on production, and community norms. Identified participant population, including extension agents, farmers, farm workers, and farm safety and community organizations that have expressed an interest in supporting and extending the intervention beyond the current agreement (9 points).

2. Goals and Objectives (20 points)

   The extent to which specific research questions and/or hypotheses are described. The extent to which the applicant has included goals which are relevant to the purpose of reducing injuries, illnesses, and/or hazard exposure to agricultural workers and the specific problem addressed by the applicant.

   The extent to which the applicant has included goals and objectives that are specific, measurable, time-phased, feasible to be accomplished during the budget period, and which address all activities necessary to accomplish the purpose of the proposal.

   The extent to which objectives include involving agricultural workers, communities, and other stakeholders in the planning, implementation and evaluation of the intervention.

3. Methods (25 points)

The extent to which the applicant provides a detailed description of overall design and methods selected for the intervention(s) including the designation of responsibility for each action undertaken.

The extent to which the target population and setting in which the intervention is to be implemented are clearly described and shown to be adequate for achieving the desired objectives.

The extent to which it is demonstrated that the participation of the target group will be sufficient to evaluate the intervention in an unbiased fashion.

The extent to which the applicant has met the CDC policy requirements regarding the inclusion of women, ethnic, and racial groups in the proposed research. This includes: (a) The proposed plan for the inclusion of both sexes and racial and ethnic minority populations for appropriate representation; (b) The proposed justification when representation is limited or absent; (c) A statement as to whether the design of the study is adequate to measure differences when warranted; and (d) A statement as to whether the plans for recruitment and outreach for study participants include the process of establishing partnerships with community(ies) and recognition of mutual benefits will be documented.

4. Staffing, Facilities and Resources (15 points total)

a. The extent to which organizational structure, job descriptions, proposed staffing, staff qualifications and experience, identified training needs or plan, and curricula vitae for both the proposed and current staff indicate the applicant's ability to carry out the objectives of the program. The extent to which the management staff and their working partners are clearly described, appropriately assigned and have pertinent skills and experiences, e.g., previous accomplishments in agricultural safety and health interventions. Time allocation of the professional staff to be assigned to this project (8 points).

b. The extent to which concurrence with the applicant's plans by all other involved parties is specific and documented, e.g., support for proposed activities as well as commitment to participate from proposed partners (e.g., letters of support and/or memoranda of understanding). The extent to which the participants are clearly described and their qualifications for their components of the proposed work are explicitly stated. The extent to which the applicant provides proof of the involvement of partners/stakeholders (e.g., agricultural workers, agricultural organizations, agribusiness) in the development of this proposal (7 points).

5. Evaluation (20 points)

The extent to which the proposed evaluation system is detailed and will document program process, effectiveness, impact, and outcome. The extent to which an evaluation plan has been developed to determine both the success of the pilot intervention or demonstration project(s) and to determine its utility as a public health prevention strategy with broader application in other communities. The extent to which the applicant demonstrates potential data sources for evaluation purposes, and documents staff availability, expertise, and capacity to perform the evaluation. The extent to which a feasible plan for reporting evaluation results and using evaluation information for programmatic decisions is included.

6. Budget and Justification (not scored)

The extent to which the applicant provides a detailed budget and narrative justification consistent with stated objectives and planned program activities.

7. Human Subjects Review (not scored)

The applicant must clearly state what precautions will be taken to protect human subjects.

I. Other Requirements

Technical Reporting Requirements

Provide CDC with original plus two copies of:

1. annual progress reports;

2. financial status report, no more than 90 days after the end of the budget period; and

3. final financial and performance reports, no more than 90 days after the end of the project period.

Send all reports to: Sheryl Heard, Grants Management Specialist, Grants Management Branch, Procurement and Grants Office, Centers for Disease Control and Prevention (CDC), 2920 Brandywine Road, Mail Stop E13, Atlanta, GA 30341.

The following additional requirements are applicable to this program. For a complete description of each, see Attachment I in the application package.

AR-1   Human Subjects Requirements
AR-2   Requirements for Inclusion of Women and Racial and Ethnic Minorities in Research
AR-9   Paperwork Reduction Act Requirements
AR-10 Smoke-Free Workplace Requirements
AR-11 Healthy People 2000
AR-12 Lobbying Restrictions

Authority and Catalog of Federal Domestic Assistance Number

This program is authorized under section 20(a) and 22(e)(7) of the Occupational Safety and Health Act of 1970, (29 U.S.C. 669(a) and 671(e)(7)). The Catalog of Federal Domestic Assistance number is 93.283.

J. Where To Obtain Additional Information

Please refer to Program Announcement 990IJ9 when you request information. To receive additional written information and to request an application kit, call 1-888-GRANTS4 (1-888-472-6874). You will be asked to leave your name and address and will be instructed to identify the Announcement number of interest.

See also the CDC home page on the Internet: ***http://www.cdc.org***

If you have questions after reviewing the contents of all the documents, please contact: Sheryl Heard, Grants Management Specialist, Grants Management Branch, Procurement and Grants Office, Announcement 99039, Centers for Disease Control and Prevention 920 Brandywine Road, Mail Stop E-13, Atlanta, GA 30341.

For program technical assistance, contact Ionet Ehlers, R.N., M.S.N., Occupational Health Nurse, National Institute for Occupational Safety and Health (NIOSH), Centers for Disease Control and Prevention (CDC). Division of Surveillance, Hazard Evaluations and Field Studies, 4676 Columbia Parkway, R-21, Cincinnati, OH 45226 or Teri Palermo, R.N. Public Health Advisor, NIOSH/CDC, Division of Respiratory Disease Studies, Office of the Director, 1095 Willowdale Road, Mailstop 127, Morgantown, WV 26505-2888.

Diane D. Porter, Acting Director, National Institute for Occupational Safety and Health Centers for Disease Control and Prevention (CDC). (FR Doc. 99-3197 Filed 2-9-99; 8:45 am)

BILLING CODE 4163-19-P

Keycode	Keyword
A001900	Centers for Disease Control
0201000	Agriculture
020100A	All Agriculture
0200000	Agriculture & Food Sciences & Foods
0730070	Public Health
073000A	All Health Care
0700000	Health & Safety, Medical & Biomedical Sciences
0000034	Research
0730000	Health Care
0201028	Form & Ranch Management
725020	Occupational Health and Safety
072500A	All Environment (Health & Safety & Medical)
0725005	Environmental Health
0725000	Environment (Health & Safety & Medical)
074500A	All Intervention, Types of (Health Safety & Medical)
0745000	Intervention, Types of (Health & Safety & Medical)
0715027	Injury
071500A	All Disease Entities & Medical Problems & Behavior
0715000	Disease Entities & Medical Problems

Foundation

The James S. McDonnell Foundation

Program for Collaborative Pilot Projects in Cognitive Rehabilitation Research. This RFP contains all the information needed to prepare a proposal for submission. Individuals seeking clarification on the information provided in this RFP are encouraged to contact the Foundation via e-mail, when possible. Contact information is provided in the body of the RFP.

PLEASE REVIEW THE PROGRAM DESCRIPTION CAREFULLY PRIOR TO PREPARING AN APPLICATION. Applications not meeting program guidelines will be rejected upon receipt.

For the past decade, the James S. McDonnell Foundation (JSMF) has supported research in cognitive neuroscience (the McDonnell-Pew Program in Cognitive Neuroscience) and in the application of cognitive science to educational practice (Cognitive Studies for Educational Practice). In 1996, the Foundation launched a new program combining research in cognitive neuroscience, cognitive science, and instruction to develop new strategies, applications, and learning environments for individuals participating in cognitive rehabilitation following brain injury. A description of the projects funded in 1998 can be found on this web site.

This new McDonnell Foundation program will award up to $600,000 annually in support of cognitive rehabilitation research carried out by interdisciplinary teams of cognitive neuroscientists, cognitive psychologists, and rehabilitation professionals. The program supports small-scale pilot projects. The work should be novel and unlikely to be funded by federal grant programs.

Proposed projects should address how the research findings on brain plasticity, brain structure/function relationships, cognitive science, studies of learning, and information processing theory can be applied to the design of clinical interventions to help individuals with brain injuries improve their performance of functional, real-world tasks (e.g., self-care, meal preparation, tasks related to employment, etc.). Research teams proposing to identify the cognitive or neurobiological substrates of functional recovery (i.e., cortical reorganization, using new cognitive strategies) with the goal of developing cognitive therapies are also appropriate for this RFP.

Preference will be given to projects that address ameliorating the cognitive deficits resulting from acquired brain damage rather than deficits resulting from developmental disorders or neurodegenerative diseases. All proposals must clearly articulate how the theories, methods, and results of cognitive science and cognitive neuroscience support and inform the proposed cognitive intervention. The proposals should also address the intervention's expected functional benefit and describe how patient's functional improvements will be measured and assessed.

The program will not consider proposals based on measuring the cognitive performance of patient and control populations with laboratory-based neuropsychological tests that do not correlate with or predict function on real-world behavioral tasks. The Foundation will not review proposals that manifest no serious intent to form interdisciplinary collaborations or that undertake no novel approaches to improving individual performance through cognitive rehabilitation strategies.

Examples of the types of proposals requested by this RFP include:

Collaborations among cognitive neuroscientists, cognitive psychologists, and rehabilitation specialists to apply findings about brain structure/function relationships in developing new therapies to treat the cognitive deficits resulting from traumatic, cerebrovascular or metabolic brain injuries. The projects must emphasize measurably improving function in everyday real-world tasks that will 1) increase the ability of the individual to live independently, resume schooling, or return to work or 2) decrease an individual's dependence on caregivers. Applicable research topics include the appropriate design and implementation of cognitive assistive devices, assessing the ability of the brain to accomplish tasks via multiple strategies, and relating the time courses of neurological, neurophysiological and neurochemical recovery to the recovery of behavioral function.

Collaborations between cognitive psychologists studying learning and rehabilitation professionals to adapt cognitively based educational interventions for use in rehabilitation settings. Typical projects would include 1) using technology, as either learning aids or long-term cognitive assistive devices, to enhance function on real-world everyday tasks, 2) adapting the tenets of cognitive science and cognitive psychology to structure rehabilitation environments to facilitate learning, and 3) applying what is known about learning in special populations (e.g. mentally retarded, learning disabled) to persons with acquired brain damage. The projects must be grounded in learning theories firmly based in cognitive science and cognitive psychology.

Support may be requested for the activities described below. Proposals must:

1. Clearly indicate in what ways the proposed research represents a new approach to cognitive rehabilitation, and;

2. Identify the cognitive neuroscience and cognitive science findings on which the project is based.

Institutional or inter-institutional collaborative groups working together as multi-disciplinary teams as described in this RFP can request up to $60,000 over two years to support innovative pilot projects. The proposals should request funding for pilot studies only. There will be no grant support for partial funding of large scale, ongoing research programs. Projects must submit progress reports at the end of the first year and at the end of the funding period. The second year of funding is contingent on the Foundation receiving an acceptable report at the end of the first year. Letters of commitment to the collaborative project from each of the project participants must be attached to the proposal.

Application Guidelines

NOTE: Applications not meeting the specifications described below will be rejected without review by the program advisory board. Please follow all word limit specifications. Proposals should be double-spaced and should be in no less than 12 pt type. Advisors review many applications within a short time period. Applications that are well-organized and easy to read have an obvious advantage.

Each proposal must contain:

1. A cover sheet providing the proposal's descriptive title, the proposed start date, the name of the institution to which the grant would be made, the names and positions of the principal investigator(s), and the name and contact information for the university administrator responsible for administering the grant. The principal investigator serving as the contact for the proposal must provide a complete mailing address, phone number, and e-mail address.

2. A 500-word abstract understandable to a general, non-scientific audience.

3. A narrative description of the proposed study group activities or the pilot project not exceeding 5000 words (not including references).

4. A detailed budget and budget justification. The budget must include a time line describing how the funds will be expended over the grant period. Please refer to *guidelines* on the Foundation's web site for additional budget information.

5. Short-form curriculum-vitae for each pilot project participant.

Proposals must be received in the Foundation office on or before the close of business, 5 PM CST, March 15. The Foundation will not review incomplete or late proposals and no exceptions will be made.

Receipt of proposals will only be acknowledged if a self-addressed, stamped postcard with, pre-printed acknowledgement message is provided with the application package.

The Foundation anticipates that the grants will be awarded by the end of June.

Address proposals to: Susan M. Fitzpatrick, Ph.D., Program Officer, James S. McDonnell Foundation, 1034 S. Brentwood Blvd., Suite 1850, St. Louis, Missouri 63117.

Direct questions concerning this RFP to susan@jsmf.org. We prefer that you use e-mail whenever possible. If you do not have access to the Internet or e-mail, please call 314-721-1532.

Appendix B

Sample Grant Applications

Operation Lifeline

Assessing Functional Fitness in
Sedentary and Physically Active
Older Persons: An International
Collaborative Research Project

Operation Lifeline Proposal

Abstract

Operation Lifeline is a community-based program of St. Elizabeth Medical Center (SEMC). The purpose of this program is to provide a personal emergency response system which allows frail, elderly, and disabled persons in Portage County to remain living independently in their own homes despite advanced age, chronic medical problems, or social isolation.

For the past three years, SEMC has sponsored the Operational Lifeline Program with initial funds from hospital guilds, civic and social organizations, and private donations. Through the provision of a telephone emergency alarm and response system, the program currently provides 54 individuals with a constant sense of security. If the Lifeline subscriber presses a small transmitter button which can be carried about, or if he/she shows unusual inactivity, the Lifeline system will automatically call for help to the 24-hour response base unit located in the SEMC Emergency Department.

At present levels, this emergency response system can only serve a small fraction of eligible subscribers in Portage County while the waiting list continues to grow. The number of applications for the Lifeline Service would be expected to greatly increase if publicity efforts were stepped up or if social service agencies were invited to refer their clients.

The St. Elizabeth Community Health Foundation is seeking funds in order to expand the Operation Lifeline Service to others, and dissolve the waiting list of eligible subscribers. We are asking the Glaser Foundation for $25,000 to provide ongoing financial support necessary to operate and expand the program. This fund request will enable us to meet a greater percentage of the need that is evident in the Portage community. Specific funding includes the purchase of 30 additional Lifeline units, the cost of one part-time personnel to keep up with expansion demands, and operational costs not covered by the eight dollar monthly subscriber fees.

I. Introduction

St. Elizabeth Medical Center, now in its 93rd year of service to the Portage Valley, is operated under the sponsorship of the Sisters of Providence, headquartered in Seattle. The 189-bed hospital is a recognized nonprofit, tax-exempt organization. Operation Lifeline is viewed as a natural outgrowth of the Sisters' Mission, which reflects a principal commitment to the care of poor and elderly.

Operation Lifeline is a protective human service with the program goal of providing a personal emergency response system that enables lower income, disabled, and socially isolated elderly persons to maintain an independent living situation. The Lifeline equipment provides 24-hour access to emergency medical help at the press of a button. Each of the 54 subscribers have a Lifeline communicator/unit at home with a portable button that can be worn on clothing or carried around the house in a pocket. At the first sign of trouble, the "at risk" person can push the button. This sends an electronic message via the telephone to the SEMC Emergency Department where trained personnel arrange for help. The Lifeline equipment even has the ability to send a signal for help when the subscriber is unconscious. (Please refer to Appendix A for further Lifeline System information).

Operation Lifeline has proven to be reliable and effective. Subscribers have used the equipment in cases of heart attacks, falls, strokes, emotional distress, robbery and assault. Many emergencies occur at night

when there is no help available in the home, and neighbors are asleep. There are approximately 50 emergencies expected for every 100 users.

Operation Lifeline has saved lives in Portage County. One recent emergency was incurred by a 59 year old subscriber who lives alone and has severe respiratory problems, which were complicated one morning by a viral infection she had contracted. When she found it too difficult to breathe, she pressed her personal HELP-button which relayed the message for help to the SEMC Emergency Department. A nurse at the Response Center called the subscriber's first responder (a neighbor) who went quickly to her home, evaluated the situation, and then called an ambulance. The entire process took only seven minutes. From her hospital bed, the subscriber agreed that the Lifeline System is a lifesaver. "I can't imagine anything more wonderful for people like myself who live alone," she said.

II. Problem and Need

Many elderly persons suffer the multiple threats of chronic disability, poverty, social isolation, and reduced mobility. It becomes more and more difficult for them to maintain an independent lifestyle since they feel vulnerable to medical and environmental emergencies but are alone and "out of touch." Thus, many older adults are confronted with limited options that may include:

1. Institutionalization.

2. Securing daily home health care services through local agencies or homemaker help from relatives and friends.

3. Living with their unsatisfactory situations.

The cost and/or availability of institutions and service options is obviously a limiting factor; limiting in the sense that institutional care may not be affordable (or desirable) to elderly persons, and further, that home health services is generally not adequate relative to demand.

Based on 1990 Census Data, 16.7 percent or 28,913 residents of Portage County are age 60 or older. Of this total, 24 percent or 7,046 elderly persons live alone, and 35 percent of these people who live alone have incomes below the poverty level. Additionally, 5,723 people are disabled to the extent that they are prevented from working. Both elderly and disabled persons share the jeopardy of living alone on a fixed income with chronic health problems in relative isolation.

Portage County evidences a definite need to assist those elderly and disabled residents who do not possess the capability or resources to maintain an independent living situation. The assistance should be such that the individual's personal security is also maintained. The Operation Lifeline Program goals fulfill this need.

III. Objectives

The primary objectives in the operation Lifeline Program are:

1. To help low income elderly and/or disabled individuals maintain independence in their own homes with the greatest possible security, confidence, and dignity, by the addition of 30 new Lifeline Units in 1997.

2. To reduce the sense of isolation for elderly and/or disabled persons by providing a feeling of security that one can get help quickly in case of accident or

illness, by conducting in-home demonstrations to train subscribers about usage of the Lifeline System.

3. To decrease the threat of institutionalization and increase the opportunity to link frail persons at home with the full range of medical/social services available by adding a program coordinator to assure successful program operation.

4. To assure those who are socially isolated that they can receive protective emergency services in the case of crime or other environmental stress, by providing ongoing Operation Lifeline procedural information through workshops/ training to all law enforcement agencies in Portage County.

5. To increase the capability to identify needy and qualified subscribers within the community who could benefit from the Lifeline System, by continuous contact with all appropriate health services involved in providing subscriber referrals.

6. To maintain the quality of service the Lifeline subscribers now enjoy even as the quantity of Lifeline units increases by monitoring/analyzing documented reports provided by the SEMC Emergency Department to assure a long term individual case management approach.

IV. Methods and Activities

The purpose of Operation Lifeline is to provide a personal emergency response system for low income, disabled, and socially isolated elderly persons to maintain an independent lifestyles, and there are three functional components designed to achieve this goal. These components, performed throughout the program include administering the program, installation and maintenance of Lifeline equipment, and the emergency response center monitoring.

1. Program Administration Activities

   a. The program director will implement a process of participant recruitment, insuring that all eligible persons are made aware of and encouraged to participate in program services for 30 new subscribers.

   b. The program director will receive inquiries and determine needy clients through a screening and selection process according to established criteria (health status, income, residence, and degree of isolation).

   c. The program director will establish and provide linkages with all appropriate social service agencies, medical facilities, and media to notify in case of available Lifeline units (i.e., verbal and written contact).

   d. The program coordinator will schedule intake visits with new subscribers and secure rental agreements.

   e. The program coordinator will schedule volunteers for conducting in-home demonstrations to train user and emergency first responders (family, friends and neighbors) about the Lifeline System, and to make monthly contact calls.

   f. The program coordinator will order installation of Lifeline units for new subscribers.

g. The program coordinator will respond to questions and problems of subscriber, Lifeline installer, and volunteers.

h. The St. Elizabeth Community Foundation secretary will provide the billing service for all existing and new subscribers.

i. The SEMC Education Department secretary will prepare and send notifications of installations, repairs, and removals as well as quarterly Operation Lifeline Newsletters to all subscribers.

j. Trained volunteers will provide in-home demonstrations of the Lifeline System to train the user and emergency first responders (family, friends, and neighbors); and make monthly contact with each subscriber to review and evaluate status, and to test each system.

2. Installation and Maintenance

a. The volunteer installer will receive orders and schedules of installations and coordinate time of Lifeline unit installation with program coordinator.

b. The volunteer will respond to repair and removal requests immediately, and perform systematic testing when necessary.

c. The volunteer will provide technical training to additional volunteers on installation, removal, and testing procedures.

3. Emergency Response Center

a. SEMC Emergency Department will provide and train personnel to monitor the Lifeline base unit with 24 hours, 7 days/week coverage.

b. SEMC Emergency Department personnel will decode emergency signals and initiate an emergency plan on the Lifeline subscriber's behalf.

c. SEMC Emergency Department personnel will monitor outcome and maintain incident/outcome documentation.

d. SEMC Emergency Department personnel will participate in equipment testing.

e. SEMC Emergency Department will be responsible for base unit maintenance and repair.

Through the provisions of the requested funds from the Glaser Foundation, Operation Lifeline will implement a specific time line of events to accomplish the stated objective of expanding services to meet the growing needs of the low income elderly, disabled and socially isolated population of Portage County.

The proposed time line of increasing subscriber Lifeline units is as follows:

1. By September 1, 1997, the program director will disseminate information about 30 additional Lifeline units.

2. By September 30, 1997, the program director will begin the screening and selection process of new applicants according to Lifeline subscriber criteria.

3. By September 30, 1997, volunteer Lifeline equipment installers will provide technical training to additional recruited volunteers on installation procedures.

4. By October 15, 1997, the program coordinator will start scheduling intake visits with new subscribers and secure rental agreements.

5. By October 31, 1997 the program coordinator will schedule volunteers to conduct in-home training demonstrations for 10 new subscribers and first responders about the Lifeline unit functions and procedures in conjunction with equipment installation.

6. By November 30, 1997, the program coordinator will schedule volunteers to conduct in-home training demonstrations for 10 new subscribers and first responders about the Lifeline unit functions and procedures in conjunction with equipment installation.

7. By January 1, 1998, the program coordinator will schedule volunteers to conduct in-home training demonstrations for the remaining 10 new subscribers and first responders about the Lifeline unit functions and procedures in conjunction with equipment installation.

8. Monthly telephone calls to subscribers by trained volunteers will be conducted to test each system as well as to review and evaluate present status.

9. By July 15 1998, the program director will disseminate survey questionnaires to subscribers, community service organizations providing referrals, and program personnel/volunteers.

10. By August 30 1998, the program director will evaluate satisfaction and the effectiveness of Operation Lifeline.

The proposed timeline for additional personnel follows:

1. By September 1, 1997, the program director will advertise for a part-time program coordinator staff position (.25 FTE).

2. By September 29, 1997, the program director will complete the selection process of program coordinator applicants.

3. By October 1, 1997, the program director will begin orienting new employees to the program coordinator position.

4. Monthly staff meetings will be conducted to provide ongoing training of the Operation Lifeline service, as well as staff the subscriber cases of reported emergency calls.

V. Evaluation

While expansion efforts are underway to accomplish the objectives of helping low income elderly, disabled and socially isolated individuals maintain an independent lifestyle, Operation Lifeline will continue to strive for optimal quality of service. The SEMC Educational Services Department will maintain evaluative responsibility by:

1. Monitoring/analyzing documented reports of the emergency response center in terms of emergencies and how they were handled, life-saving effectiveness, and quality control.

2. Making monthly telephone call checks to subscribers by trained volunteers, serving to retrain the subscriber in the use of the service if necessary, or to detect any problems that may need professional follow up.

3. Surveying to assess satisfaction as well as effectiveness of the service in meeting the needs of the subscriber at the end of the program year, designed for the subscriber as well as those providing the Operation Lifeline Service.

V. Continuation of Service

The Lifeline equipment is expected to provide a minimum of eight to ten years of service and can be used with many different clients, some for short periods during convalescent recovery and others for long-term periods. Once the equipment is purchased, the cost to maintain the program is relatively small, and is partially offset by the eight dollar per month subscriber fees.

When a subscriber no longer needs the Lifeline unit, the unit becomes the property of Operation Lifeline. Therefore it can be removed and reinstalled into the home of a new subscriber. Since these units usually last longer than the average subscriber's need, this assures maximum equipment utilization at minimal cost to the elderly.

VII. Future Funding

Because Operation Lifeline relies primarily on hardware (Lifeline units/equipment), the funding directly affects the number of needy people served. Presently, the program has been scaled down to the level of funding available. However, it is anticipated that the need is so great for the emergency response systems that provide an independent lifestyle for thousands of elderly and disabled individuals living alone in Portage County that in addition to the $25,000 request, we will need $50,000 (60 units) in the next two years.

Summary

There is a critical need in Portage County to provide cost effective alternatives to vulnerable individuals threatened with institutionalization or unsatisfactory living conditions. Operation Lifeline addresses this need — the isolation and vulnerability of many elderly persons who are trying to maintain themselves independently in our community despite disability, poverty, lack of social support and sometimes dangerous living conditions.

Under the sponsorship of St. Elizabeth Medical Center (SEMC) Operation Lifeline currently serves 54 eligible subscribers. The program consists of mostly SEMC donated personnel and dedicated volunteers who plan and implement direct services to the subscribers. Specific implementation of the program includes administration, installation and maintenance of Lifeline equipment, and the emergency response center monitoring.

Volunteers are a vital part of Operation Lifeline. The monthly follow-up calls by three volunteers and the volunteer Lifeline installer maintain the spirit of personal caring. They add sensitivity and patience while lessening the social isolation for the elderly/disabled person, and the subscriber can sense that their involvement is a personal commitment.

The nature of this program is such that a large proportion of funds necessary to expand Operation Lifeline is the capital expenditure of one-time related costs (Lifeline equipment). The St. Elizabeth Community Foundation is requesting $25,000 which will enable this program to meet a greater percentage of the need that has been demonstrated for this service.

The one year expansion of this program includes additional personnel, 30 Lifeline units, and various other costs for successful program implementation and identification of needy individuals. Future funding after this initial year of expansion will be considered in 1998.

Figure 13. Sample Budget

Budget Summary 1997-98

	Total Requested	Total Donated	Total
Personnel			
A. Salaries & Wages	$5,280.00	$19,872.00	$25,152.00
B. Fringe Benefits	2,106.72	7,795.89	9,902.61
C. Consultant Services		1,728.60	1,728.60
Non-Personnel			
D. Space Costs	615.00		615.00
E. Purchase of Equipment	14,490.00		14,490.00
F. Consumable Supplies	1,070.00	200.00	1,270.00
G. Travel	184.44	184.56	369.00
H. Contractual	300.00	600.00	900.00
I. Telephone		130.00	130.00
J. Other Costs	1,569.00		1,569.00
Total this Grant	**$25,000.16**	**$31,126.05**	**$56,126.21**
Indirect Costs 25% Chargeable to the Award	$6,250.00		

	Total Requested	Total Donated	Total
A. SALARY & WAGES, PERSONNEL			
A-1 Program Director (.20 FTE X $1,760 X12 mos.)	$4,224.00		$4,224.00
A-2 Program Coordinator (.25 FTE X $1,760 X 12 mos.)	5,280.00		5,280.00
A-3 Program Secretary (.5 FTE X $1,256 X 12 mos.)		$7,536.00	7,536.00
A-4 Program Billing Secretary (.5 FTE X $1,256 X 12 mos.)		7,536.00	7,536.00
A-5 ER Nursing Staff (4 hrs/mo X $12/hr X 12 mos.)		576.00	576.00
TOTAL PERSONNEL	**$528.00**	**$19,872.00**	**$25,152.00**
B. FRINGE BENEFITS			
B-6 SEMC Staff 39.9%	$2,106.72	$7,699.10	$9,805.82
B-7 SEMC Nurses 18.4%		96.79	96.79
C. CONSULTANT SERVICES			
C-8 Volunteers (43 hrs./mo X $3.35/hr X 12 mos.)	$1,728.60	$1,728.60	
D. SPACE COSTS			
D-9 Office Rent (.50 X $1,231/yr)		$615.50	$615.50

continued on page 86

continued from page 85

	Total Requested	Total Donated	Total
E. PURCHASE OF EQUIPMENT			
E-10 Lifeline Units ($483/unit X 30)	$14,190.00		$14,490.00
F. CONSUMABLE SUPPLIES			
F-11 Glaser Foundation Engrave Nameplates ($9 ea. X 30 units)	$270.00		$270.00
F-12 Jack Adapters ($5 ea. X 10 units)	50.00		50.00
F-13 Reprogram to Dial-1 ($15 X 10 units)	150.00		150.00
F-14 Belt Clip ($1 X 10 units)	10.00		10.00
F-15 Help Button ($40 ea. X 10)		$400.00	400.00
F-16 Battery ($15 ea. X 10)	150.00		150.00
F-17 Instructional Subscriber Pamphlets ($30/200 quantity)	30.00		30.00
F-18 Subscriber Info Cards ($10/100 quantity)	10.00		10.00
F-19 Office Supplies		200.00	200.00
G. TRAVEL			
G-20 Local Mileage for Lifeline Installer (150 mi./mo. @ .205/mi. X 12 mos.)	$184.44	$184.56	$369.00
H. CONTRACTUAL			
H-21 Base Unit Maintenance Contract with SEMC Emergency Department ($300/yr-10/1/86-9/30/87)	$300.00		$300.00
H-22 Lifeline Unit Installer ($15/hr X 40 units)		$600.00	600.00
I. TELEPHONE			
I-23 (1) Instrument & Service		$130.00	$130.00
J. OTHER			
J-24 Printing (PR, evaluation survey & $1,469.00 misc. material)	$1,469.00		$1,469.00
J-25 Postage (Letters, survey forms, misc.)	100.00		100.00
K. TOTAL DIRECT COST			
K-26 Direct Costs	$25,000.00	$25,570.81	$54,570.81
L. TOTAL INDIRECT COST			
L-27 St. Elizabeth Community Health Foundation (25% of direct cost)	$6,250.00	$7,392.70	$13,642.70
M. TOTALS			
M-28 Total Direct and Indirect Charges	$31,250.00	$36,963.00	$68,213.51

BUDGET ADDENDUM
Category Line Item Explanation
Operation Lifeline

A-1 The program director for Operation Lifeline is Cindy Norwood. Ms. Norwood has served as the Community Health Promotion Coordinator for the SEMC Education Services Department for the past year and a half. She has a strong background in planning and implementing a variety of health programs. She will carry the responsibility of directing the overall program administration and evaluation phase as .2 FTE for Operation Lifeline.

A-2 The program coordinator position is currently being filled by Kari Baldwin, an intern from Kent State University, with major studies in Community Health Education and Social Services. The appointment is on a three month summer basis, and at the end of her appointment, Ms. Baldwin will be offered this position. However, in the event of her departure, a .25 FTE on program funds will be filled for this position that will continue Ms. Baldwin's responsibilities. The program coordinator will carry out the day-to-day implementation of Operation Lifeline as well as supervising and providing direction for all volunteers.

A-3 The secretary designation is a Secretary III position established on a .5 FTE basis. The position consists of duties that play a part in successful implementation of the program (i.e., all telephone calls, filing, subscriber correspondence, photocopying, program newsletters, etc.).

A-4 The program billing secretary is currently filled by Donna Burrill, secretary for the St. Elizabeth Community Health Foundation. This secretary II position is established on a .5 FTE basis and provides the entire billing/accounting service for the program.

A-5 The SEMC Emergency Department Nursing Staff provide the program with emergency response and monitoring of subscriber alarms, a critical component of direct service to the Operation Lifeline subscribers. The time spent is calculated according to time spend answering and documenting calls, follow up, and monthly equipment testing participation.

B-6 This item supports the fringe benefits package offered.

B-7 Through SEMC, the requested amount refers to benefits for .25 FTE program coordinator.

C-8 This item refers to volunteer time spent on monthly subscriber telephone calls, and in-home demonstrations of Lifeline system to subscribers and first responders.

D-9 This item accounts for total office space needed for all program personnel/volunteers, and is provided by SEMC.

E-10 Thirty subscriber units consisting of Lifeline Communicator Model H101A as a complete ready-to-install unit that represents the major expenditure of funds requested.

F-11 This item covers the cost of engraved nameplates of your foundation to be placed on 30 new Lifeline units.

F-12 to F-16 These items account for average costs of replacement on a yearly basis for 84 total units.

F-17 and F-18 These items represent needed supplies for direct service to subscribers.

F-19 This item accounts for basic program supplies (i.e., pens, pencils, typewriter ribbon, paper products, etc., donated by SEMC).

G-20 Program travel is based on the average mileage of installer for new installations/removals of current number of Lifeline units, as well as travel for installation of

30 additional units per year. A local community service organization donates up to $15.38/mo., and the remaining travel costs are requested.

H-21 This item concerns a service contract with SEMC Emergency Department to repair/maintain the Base Unit Lifeline equipment on a yearly basis; costs are requested.

H-22 This is an estimation of amount paid for an installer with technical training and knowledge of the current volunteer installer. The estimated installer time spent includes new installations/removals of current number of Lifeline units, as well as installation of 30 additional units.

I-23 This item is donated by SEMC.

J-24 This item accounts for all PR costs as well as evaluation surveys and other miscellaneous material.

K-26 The figure represents SEMC/Glaser Foundation support for Operation Lifeline. This is to complement the requested amount of support from the Glaser Foundation. Total direct charges for Operation Lifeline are $54,570.81.

L-27 Twenty-five percent (25%) of direct charges is the standard used by St. Elizabeth Community Health Foundation (please refer to attached Appendix B) and is consistent with Federal rules and regulations.

M-28 Total direct and indirect charges for Operation Lifeline.

The Lifeline System

Lifeline was designed by Professor Andrew Dibner, a Boston University specialist in rehabilitation and gerontology. The system was studied and tested in a three-year $640,000 grant provided by U.S. Department of Health, Education, and Welfare research grant.

Lifeline is a system consisting of:

1. Home unit electronic equipment

2. A response center monitor located in the SEMC Emergency Department

3. Neighborhood First Responders

These combined features reduce isolation and provide 24-hour emergency response.

A wireless call button is owned by the subscriber. When help is needed, the button is pressed and the Lifeline Communicator (within 200 feet) receives the wireless signal, captures the phone line (even if the telephone is off the hook), and sends a digital message to the Emergency Response Center where it is automatically printed.

At SEMC's Emergency Department, a staff member reads the subscriber code from printed tape and retrieves the subscriber information card with name, address, telephone number, a brief statement of medical or physical problems, and a list of responders. These responders are designated by the subscriber at the time Lifeline is installed. Included are people with whom the subscriber is comfortable and who have indicated their willingness to respond in the event of an emergency. Also on the list are multiple response agencies, such as police and ambulance, which would be dispatched in the event that the volunteers were unavailable.

The Emergency Department nurse immediately places a call to the subscriber. If the subscriber can get to the telephone, the nurse evaluates what may be needed. The nurse can then determine the proper response having all the information in terms of subscriber's location and

service needs. If the subscriber does not answer the phone, the nurse assumes an emergency. Immediate action is taken to contact a responder who can arrive on the scene quickly.

Lifeline equipment is closed-looped in its design. Several checks are built into the system to ensure its full operation through the responder's arrival at the scene. Additionally, the responder must send an "all clear" signal to the Response Center by pressing a reset button. Throughout the operation the subscriber receives feedback to reassure him that he is "in touch" with help.

In the event that the subscriber is unconscious and unable to press the reset button, a clock-timer in the Lifeline home unit will initiate an emergency call. The time is set for 12 or 24 hours. It is reset manually by the subscriber pushing a reset button on the unit. Lifting the telephone handset during normal use also auto-matically resets the timer. Monthly phone calls to the subscriber to test the system reinforces the feeling of being "in touch." Operation Lifeline in its entirety reassures subscribers that they are never alone — they can get help if they need it.

Assessing Functional Fitness in Sedentary and Physically Active Older Persons: An International Collaborative Research Project

Project Director

Wojtek J. Chodzko-Zajko, Ph.D.
Kent State University
USA
Tel: (330) 672 2930
Fax: (330) 672 4106
E-Mail: Japa@kentvm.kent.edu

Participating Organizations

Kent State University, Kent, Ohio, USA
California State University - Fullerton, Fullerton, California, USA
EGREPA, The European Group for Research into Elderly and Physical Activity

Overview of the Project

An international collaborative research project is proposed to examine the relationship between regular physical activity and functional fitness in European older adults. The data collected in the present study will be compared to existing data which have recently been compiled in North American samples in Fullerton, California (Rikli and Jones, 1999a; Rikli and Jones, 1999b) and Kent, Ohio (Miofto, Chodzko-Zajko, Reich and Supler, 1999).

The goal of this study is to generate European data to add and compare with the existing United States data set. The European Group for Research into Elderly and Physical Activity (EGREPA) has provided the Principal Investi-gator with an extraordinary opportunity to train researchers to collect functional fitness data in five different European testing locations. Specifi-cally, EGREPA is prepared to dedicate a keynote address and two workshops during their 1999 Annual meeting for the training of research personnel. The selected personnel would then return to their respective laboratories to collect data. Data would subsequently be forwarded to the Principal Investigator's laboratory for data entry, collation, and analysis. Preliminary results would be presented in the 2000 EGREPA annual meeting. Ultimately, the goal of the study would be the publication of a multi-national collaborative study in the *Journal of Aging and Physical Activity*.

Following appropriate training, each of the five European investigators would be responsible for the collection of FFT data in their home country. At each data collection site, one hundred older persons (50 regularly active; 50 sedentary) will be tested. The goal of the study is to (1) establish functional fitness levels of physically active and sedentary individuals at each testing site, and (2) to compare functional fitness levels across the five European locations, and (3) to compare functional fitness levels between North America and Europe.

We propose to assess functional fitness using a new seven item Functional Fitness Test Battery (FFT, Rikli and Jones, 1999a) which has been designed to permit the objective quantification of functional capacity in a broad range of older individuals. The FFT battery is designed to maximize the discriminating power of test items within each of seven domains of functional fitness, i.e., (1) Lower Body Muscle Endurance, (2) Upper Body Muscle Strength, (3) Lower Body Flexibility, (4) Upper Body Flexibility, (5) Physical Agility, Gait, and Balance, (6) Cardiovascular Endurance, and (7) Anaerobic Power and Dynamic Balance.

Our goal is to assess the functional performance of 50 physically active and 50 sedentary older persons at each research site. At each site we will determine the functional fitness of a typical cohort of physically active seniors and compare these individuals with a cohort of sedentary persons.

In total, new data will be available on 500 subjects. Data will be pooled from each research laboratory and national and regional comparisons will be drawn.

The following research questions will be addressed:

- Are there differences in functional status between physically active and sedentary older persons?

- Are there cross-cultural differences between laboratories with respect to the functional status of physically active and sedentary persons? (For example, are Northern European sedentary older persons more or less functionally fit than a comparable group of American Seniors?)

1. Need for the study

The presence of considerable variability among older adults with respect to their underlying functional abilities is often referred to as one of the most important characteristics of aging. Spirduso (1995) has proposed that the older adult population can be categorized along a 5-point physical functioning continuum (see figure 1).

Figure 14. The Physical Functioning Continuum

Frail	Dependent	Independent	Fit	Elite

In Spirduso's model, physically fit and elite older adults are located at one end of the continuum, whereas, physically frail and dependent seniors are placed at the other end of the continuum. The largest single group in the physical functioning continuum are the sedentary and independently living cohort. These individuals do not exercise regularly and frequently have one or more chronic disease(s) that challenge them physically. However, despite these limitations, they are generally able to live independently within the community.

Both the U.S. Surgeon General's Report (1996) and the WHO guidelines (1996) recognize that the benefits of regular physical activity are not restricted to a particular group along the physical functioning continuum, but that significant benefits can be gained from physical activity by almost all older persons regardless of their health status and functional ability. For example, the WHO guidelines (1996) suggest that exercise and regular physical activity can help the fit and elite groups maintain their high levels of fitness and functional capacity. Similarly, regular physical activity is important for the sedentary group in order to maintain independence and control chronic disease. Engagement in physical activity can have significant benefits on the quality of life for the frail and dependent groups by preventing or minimizing further decline, and by increasing functional reserve so that daily activities are more easily performed and some independence is restored.

While there is some degree of understanding about the effects of physical activity within each group along the physical functioning continuum, much less is known about the factors which influence transitions between one point on the continuum and another (Chodzko-Zajko, 1996). For example, little is known about the factors which precipitate an individual's transition from the sedentary and independent category to the physically frail group. Some sedentary people can maintain an independent lifestyle for many decades, whereas, others regress far more rapidly into frailty and dependency. Several gerontologists have suggested that our understanding of the temporal dynamics of aging is unlikely to be improved until more sensitive measures of functional fitness are developed (Rikli and Jones, in press; Chodzko-Zajko, 1996). For

example, at the onset of a 25 year longitudinal study of physical activity and aging, a relatively healthy sixty year old person is likely to be able to complete all or almost all of a battery of traditional laboratory fitness tests. However, by the end of the study, at age 85, the same individual may no longer be able to safely participate in the same test battery. Because no tests exist which are sufficiently sensitive to measure functional fitness across multiple stages of the physical functioning continuum, at present there would be little option but to drop this individual from the longitudinal investigation.

Both Chodzko-Zajko (1996) and Rikli and Jones (in press) have argued that the absence of functional fitness measures that are sufficiently sensitive to assess functional fitness across a large portion of the physical functioning continuum is the single largest problem in exercise gerontology.

It is generally accepted that a functional fitness battery must include multiple components of functional fitness. Rikli and Jones (in press) propose that the key components of functional fitness which underlie activities of daily living are muscular strength and endurance, aerobic endurance, flexibility, and selected motor abilities including balance, coordination, speed, agility, and power. In recent years, several fitness batteries have been constructed in an attempt to assess functional capacity in the older adult population (Osness, Adrian, Clark, Hoeger, Raab, and Wiswell, 1987; Kim and Tanaka, 1994; Reuben and Siu, 1990). However, none of these measures have been found to adequately assess a sufficiently large range of physical abilities (Rikli and Jones, in press).

The test will be discontinued if the participant experiences pain, or shows signs of dizziness, and/or undue fatigue.

b. *Arm Curl:* This test is designed to measure arm (biceps) muscular strength and endurance (Osness et al., 1987). A stopwatch, five and eight pound hand weights (for women and men respectively), and a straight back chair will be used. Following a demonstration by the tester, a practice trial of two to three repetitions both with and without the weight will be given to check for proper form. The participant will be seated in the chair, back straight, feet flat on the floor, and the weight held in the dominant hand with the thumb up (handshake grip). The test will begin with the arm extended downward beside the chair and straight. At a signal "go", the participant will curl the arm through a full range of motion and return to the fully extended position. The examiner will stand next to the participant on the dominant arm side, placing his/her fingers lightly on the subject's mid biceps to assure that a full curl is made (subject's forearm will squeeze the examiner's fingers). The participant will be encouraged to execute as many curls as possible within a 30 second time period, but always using controlled movements during both the concentric and eccentric phases. The examiner will monitor the participant's form to be sure that the weight is carried through the full range of motion, full extension and flexion. Each correct curl will be counted, with verbal reminders given to correct improper form. If necessary, the examiner may also need to position his/her left hand beside the chair at the point of full extension so that the participant will know when full

extension has been reached. The score will be the total number of curls made correctly within the 30 second time limit. On test day, participants will receive at least five minutes of gentle warm-up prior to the beginning of testing. The test will be discontinued if the participant experiences pain and/or undue fatigue.

c. *6-Minute Walk:* This test is designed to measure aerobic endurance (Rikli and Jones, in press). Equipment will include a stopwatch, cones, popsicle sticks, tape, and a measured walking course that is marked out every five yards. The test will involve a continuous walk for six minutes, or for as long as possible up to six minutes, along the walking course. Participants will walk around the measured course, trying to cover as much distance as possible without stopping. The parameters of the walking course will be marked with cones and the five yard segments with tape. The walking area will be well lit and the surface non-slippery and level. The test will be given in a large gym and the course will be rectangular. The participants will be instructed to continuously walk around the measured course for nine minutes and to try to cover as much distance as possible without stopping. The participants will be told to pace themselves because this is not a maximal test and they should not end the test exhausted or unduly fatigued. To keep track of the laps completed by a participant, a popsicle stick will be given to the participant each time he/she passes the starting position. Participants will be tested in groups but the start times will be staggered. Participants will be told to walk alone and that they can pass other participants on the course. To assist with pacing, the participants will be told when approximately three minutes, four minutes, and five minutes have elapsed. At the end of the six minutes, participants will be told to stop and radial heart rate will be taken immediately (within five seconds) by the tester. The participants will then be asked how hard they felt they were working using the Borg RPE scale. The tester will advance the participant forward to the next five yard mark, record the mark, and count the number of popsicle sticks to determine the distance completed. The score will be the total number of yards walked in six minutes measured to the nearest five yards. For those unable to walk for the whole six minute time period, the score will be the number of yards walked before stopping. On test day, participants will be given at least five minutes of gentle warm-up prior to the beginning of the walk. The test will be discontinued if the participant shows signs of dizziness, pain, nauseousness, or undue fatigue. For safety purposes, chairs will be stationed at several points along the walk course.

d. *2-Minute Step-in-Place:* This test is designed to measure general cardiovascular condition and lower body muscle endurance (Rikli and Jones, in press). The following items will be used: a stop watch, a 30 inch piece of string, a movable elastic cord strung between two poles to indicate minimum knee height for stepping, a handheld counter, handrails, and a Borg RPE scale on a large poster. The participant will step in place raising his/her knee to a predetermined height. This knee stepping height will be at a level even with the mid-way point between the patella (middle of the knee cap) and the iliac crest (hip bone).

This point will be determined by stretching a piece of string from the patella to the iliac crest, then doubling it over to determine the mid-way point. The midway point will be marked and used to adjust the elastic cord height. Prior to the test, the examiner will demonstrate the procedure and also allow the participant to practice some steps briefly to check for understanding. At the signal "go" the participant will step in place continuously, completing as many steps as possible within the two-minute time period. A tester will count the number of steps correctly completed by the right leg using the handheld counter, and will serve as a spotter in case of loss of balance. A timer will watch the step height to assure that the participant maintains minimum knee height throughout the stepping session. Verbal reminders will be given to ensure appropriate step height. To assist with pacing the participant will be told when one minute has passed and 30 seconds are left to go. At the end of the test the participant will be asked to indicate his/ her RPE. The participants will be instructed not to continuously hold onto or lean onto the rails for support throughout the test but they may momentarily place their hands on the rails for balance. In addition, the participants will be told that their arms may, during the test, hang freely at their sides or be swung for balance, as in walking. The participants will be instructed to step so that their knees reach the height of the elastic cord every step and to make as may steps as possible in the two minutes, but to pace themselves so they do not end the test exhausted or unduly fatigued. The test score will be the number of steps taken

within two minutes. Only full steps will be counted, each time the right knee reaches the minimum height. All participants will have at least five minutes of gentle warm-up prior to the test. The test will be discontinued if at any time the participant shows signs of dizziness, pain, nausea, or undue fatigue.

e. *Sit & Reach:* This test is designed to assess lower body (primarily hamstring) flexibility (Osness et al., 1987). A yardstick and masking tape will be used. In addition, a platform approximately two by five feet and about two feet off the floor will be used instead of the floor to perform the test so the participants will not have to move up and down from the floor. The yardstick will be placed on the platform. A 12 inch strip of masking tape will be placed in position so that the 20 inch mark is exactly even with the front edge of the masking tape, the edge closest to the zero inch point. Two small pieces of tape will be placed at both ends and perpendicular to the 12 inch strip to easily mark the heel placement. Two other pieces of tape will be placed at both ends of the yardstick to hold it in place. After a demonstration by the tester, the participant will be given two practice trials followed by two test trials. The participant will sit on the platform, legs extended, with the zero end of the yardstick between the legs. The participant's heels will touch the front edge of the tape at the 20 inch mark and be 12 inches apart, the width of the 12 inch strip. The toes will be pointed straight up throughout the stretch. The tester will check that the heels remain properly positioned when the toes are up and the knees held flat on the floor. With the participant's legs straight and

hands on top of each other with fingertips even and extended, the participant slowly bends forward sliding the hands along the yardstick as far as possible. The final position, with fingertips even, must be held for two seconds. The tester will hold the participant's knees down if necessary. The score will reflect how far the middle fingertips reach on the yardstick to the nearest 1/2 inch. All test scores will be recorded. Participants will be instructed to avoid bouncing or rapid, forceful movements. Participants will be instructed to move gently and slowly and to stretch only to the point of mild discomfort, not to the point of pain.

f. *Scratch Test:* This test is designed to assess upper body and shoulder flexibility (Rikli and Jones, in press). A standard tape measure will be used. In a standing position, the participant will place the preferred hand (the hand which gives the better score, usually the dominant hand) over the same shoulder and reach as far as possible down the middle of the back, palm down and fingers extended (elbow will be pointed up). The other hand will then be placed behind the back, palm up, reaching up as far as possible in an attempt to touch or overlap, the extended middle fingers of both hands. Following a demonstration by the tester, the participant will be given two practice trials and two test trials. The tester will ensure the middle fingers of each hand are extending toward or overlapping each other as far as possible. The tester will measure the distance of overlap or the distance between the tips of the two middle fingers to the nearest 1/2 inch. Negative scores will be given to represent non-overlapping fingers, positive scores will represent overlapping fingers, and a score of zero will represent fingers that just touch but do not overlap. On test day, participants will receive five minutes of gentle warm-up prior to testing. The test will be discontinued if the participant experiences any pain.

g. *Timed "Up and Go":* This test is designed to measure physical agility and involves speed, power, coordination, and dynamic balance (Rikli and Jones, in press). A stop watch, a tape measure, a cone, and a straight back chair approximately 17 inches high will be used. The chair will be placed in a clear, well-lit, unobstructed area, facing a cone marker exactly eight feet away. The eight foot distance will be measured from the front edge of the chair to the middle of the cone. There will be at least four feet of clearance beyond the cone to allow ample turning room for the participant. The test will begin with the participant fully seated in the chair, hands on thighs, and feet flat on the floor. Following a demonstration by the tester, the participant will walk through the test one time as practice. Then the participant will be given three test trials with a 30 second rest period between trials. On the signal "go" the participant will stand up from the chair, walk as quickly as possible around the cone, and return to the chair. The participant will be instructed that this is a timed test and that the goal is to move as quickly as possible around the cone and back to the chair. The score will be the time elapsed, to the nearest tenth of a second, from the signal "go" until the participant returns to the seated position on the chair. Both test trial scores will be recorded. All participants will have 5 minutes of gentle warm-up prior to testing.

The test will be discontinued if the participant experiences any signs of dizziness or pain. The tester will also serve as a spotter, standing midway between the chair and cone, ready to assist the participant if necessary.

3. *Statistical Analysis*

All data analyses will be performed on SPSS software. ANOVA will be used to examine the ability of the functional fitness tests to discriminate between the PA and SED groups. Two way ANOVA (country by group) will be used to assess the significance of differences between testing sites.

4. *Time Course of the Study:*

**Phase One: (June 1999)
Training of European researchers, site selection**

The European researchers will be trained during two special workshops which have been scheduled during the 1999 EGREPA annual meeting which will be held in Nancy, France between June 14 and June 18, 1999.

The following individuals will be responsible for the coordination of the workshops/training protocols;

Wojtek Chodzko-Zajko, PhD *Principal*
Professor, *Investigator*
Kent State University
Editor,
Journal of Aging and Physical Activity

Roberta Rikli, PhD *Chair and Professor*
Department of Kinesiology and Health
California State University. - Fullerton

C. Jessie Jones, PhD *Director, Ruby*
Professor *Gerontology Center*
California State University - Fullerton

At the conclusion of the workshop, five European data collection sites will be chosen. Criteria for site selection will include (1) availability of appropriate laboratory facilities, (2) access to physically active and sedentary cohorts, and (3) geographic location. An attempt will be made to select sites from several geographic regions within Europe.

Phase Two: (September - December 1999) Data collection

Data will be collected in five European sites for 100 seniors in each location. Investigators Chodzko-Zajko, Rikli, and Jones will be available to assist the European site coordinators with any concerns or questions.

Phase Three: (January - May 2000) Pooling of findings

All data will be forwarded to the Principal Investigator's laboratory (Chodzko-Zajko). Chodzko-Zajko will coordinate data entry and analysis.

Phase Four: (June 2000) Initial dissemination of findings

The European and North American comparative data will be presented in a keynote symposium at the 2000 EGREPA meeting which will be held in Brussels, Belgium in June, 2000. EGREPA has agreed to provide scheduling time for the workshop.

Subsequently, a research paper based on the data will be prepared for submission to the *Journal of Aging and Physical Activity*.

5. *Budget:*

Phase One: Support is requested for three USA researchers to attend the 1999 EGREPA meeting in Nancy France in order to coordinate the training of the European research staff

Air travel to Nancy, France – economy class
$1,500 x 3 persons $4,500

EGREPA meeting registration
$350 x 3 persons $1,050

Hotel
$100 x 5 nights x 3 persons $1,500

Per diem and expense
$50 x 6 days x 3 persons $900

Phase Two: Support is requested to assist the European researchers to collect and enter data for 100 subjects per site. Support is needed for duplication costs, phone calls, minor equipment purchases, etc.

Local data collection costs, paper, duplication, phone calls, etc
$1,000 x 5 locations $5,000

Phase Three: Support is requested for the Principal Investigator to support data entry and analysis.

Data analysis and entry by PIV
$75 x 50 hours $3,750

Phase Four: Support is requested for three USA researchers and 5 European researchers attend the 1999 EGREPA meeting in Nancy, France to present the research findings in a keynote symposium.

Air travel (economy class) to Nancy, France
$1,500 x 3 persons (USA) $7,000
$500 x 5 persons (Europe)

EGREPA meeting registration
$350 x 8 persons $2,800

Hotel
$100 x 5 nights x 8 persons $4,000

Per diem and expenses
$50 x 6 days x 8 persons $2,400

Administrative Charge

The grant will be administered $1,400
by the PI through the center
for Sport and Recreation
Development at Kent State
University. The Center will
establish an account for
the project, write checks,
establish a computer account
for the study, etc. The Center's
grant administration rate
is 5 percent.

TOTAL $29,800

6. References

American College of Sports Medicine (1995), *Guidelines for Exercise Prescription and Testing*: Fifth Edition, Philadelphia, PA: Lea & Febiger.

Chodzko-Zajko, W.J. (1996). The physiology of aging: Structural changes and functional consequences: Implications for research and clinical practice in the exercise and activity sciences. *Quest*, 48 (3), 311-329.

Kim, H.S., and Tanaka, K. (1994). The assessment of functional age using "Activities of Daily Living" performance tests: A study of Korean women. *Journal of Aging and Physical Activity*, 3, 39-53.

Miofto, J.M., Chodzko-Zajko, W.J., Reich, J.L., Supler, M.M. (1999). The reliability and validity of the Fullerton Functional Fitness Test: An independent replication study. *Journal of Aging and Physical Activity*.

Osness, W.S., Adrian, M., Clark, B., Hoeger, W., Raab, D., and Wiswell, R. (1987). *Functional fitness assessment for adults over 60 years*. Reston, VA: American Alliance for Health, Physical Education, Recreation, and Dance.

Reading, T.S. and Shephard, R.J. (1992). Revision of the Physical Activity Readiness Questionnaire (PAR-Q) (based on the British Columbia Department of Health, PAR-Q Validation Report, 1975). *Canadian Journal of Sports Science*, 17, 338-345

Reuben, D.B. and Siu, A.L. (1990). An objective measure of physical function of elderly outpatients: The physical performance test. *Journal of the American Geriatrics Society*, 38, 1105-1112.

Rikli, R.R. and Jones, C.B. (1999a). Functional fitness standards for community residing adults over 60. *Journal of Aging and Physical Activity*, 7,1, in press.

Rikli, R. R. and Jones, C. B. (1999b). Assessing physical performance in "independent" older adults: Issues and guidelines. *Journal of Aging and Physical Activity*, 7,1, in press.

Spirduso, W.W. (1995). *Physical Dimensions of Aging*, Champaign, IL: Human Kinetics.

U.S. Surgeon General's Report (1996), *Physical Activity and Health*, U.S. Government Printing Office, Washington D.C.

World Health Organization (1996). The Heidelberg Guidelines for Promoting Physical Activity Among Older Persons. *Journal of Aging and Physical Activity*, 5, 1-9.